GEOMETRY OF LIFE

A Memoir in Painting

Nancy Maron

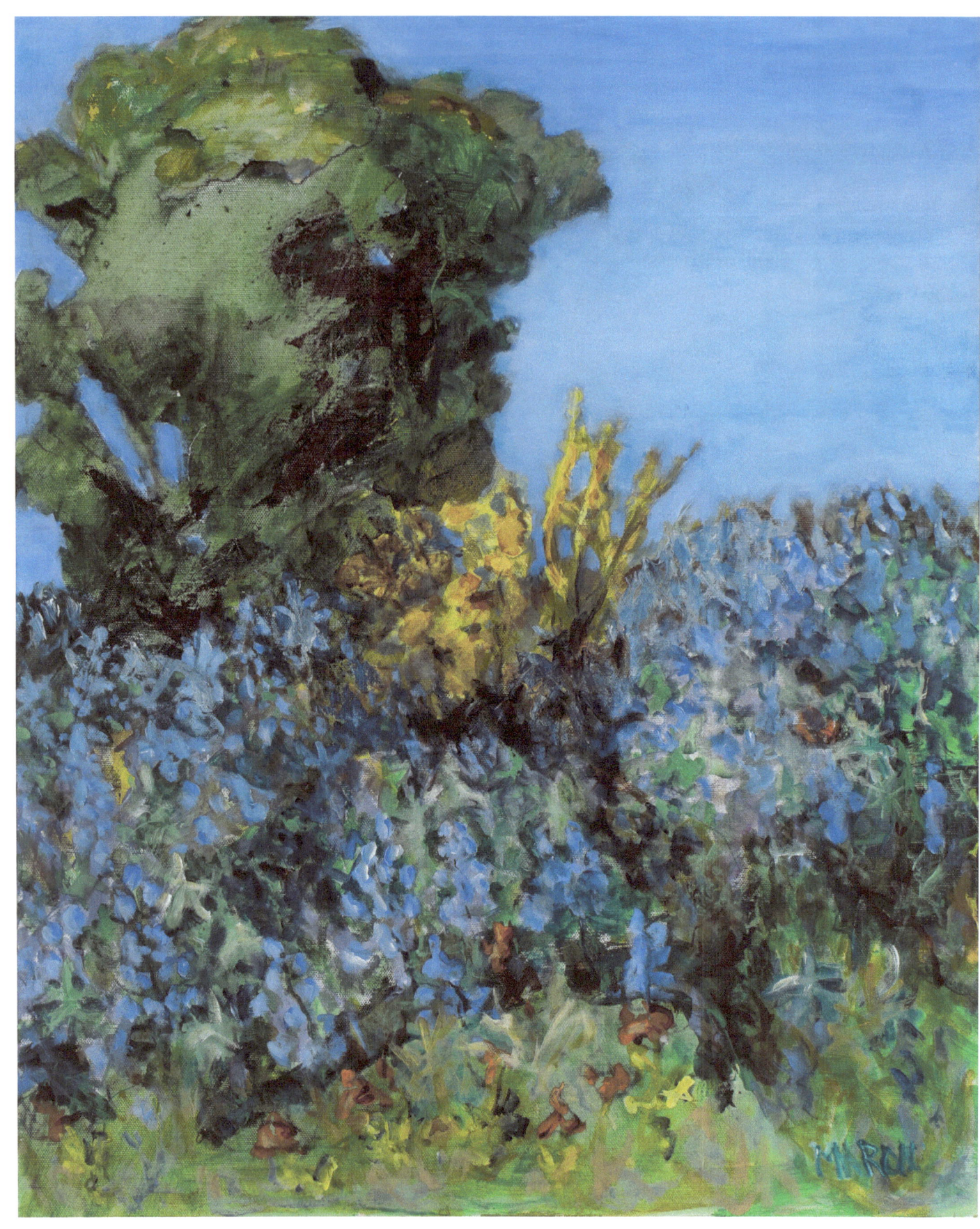

"Lupine and Madrona Tree on San Juan Island"

GEOMETRY OF LIFE

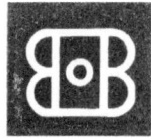

Geometry of Life: A Memoir in Painting

© Nancy Maron
nancymaronart.com

Edited by Jennifer Heath
Designed by Nora Collom
Photos and works of art © Nancy Maron
No part of this book may be reproduced with permission of the publisher

All rights reserved

Baksun Books & Arts
1838 Pine Street
Boulder, Colorado 80302 USA

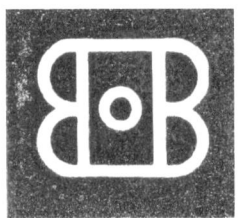

ISBN 978-1-887997-44-7

GEOMETRY OF LIFE

Made up of straight lines and angles.

Lines that cross, diverge, and sometimes dead end.

Patterns and symmetry that reoccur.

Looking back from a distance: they are discernable.

For
Larry,
my sons Bill, Jon, and Joel,
and their families

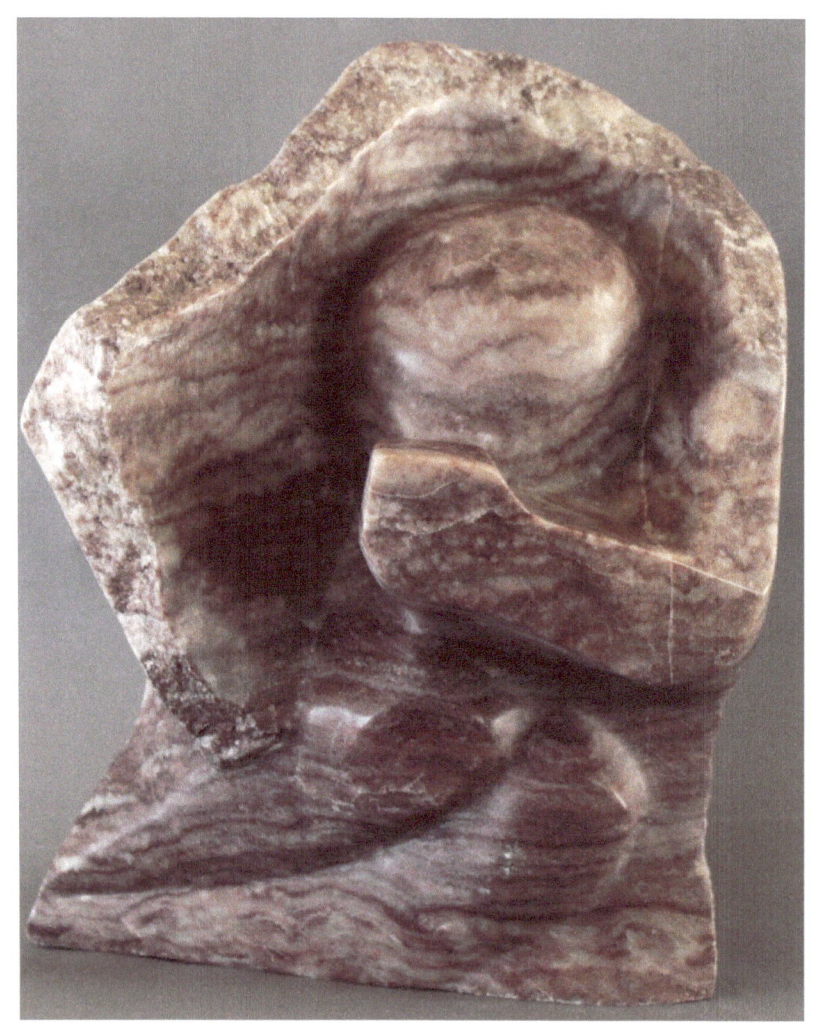

"Emergence"

Looking Through a Window

Seeing the past through a mirror or looking glass.

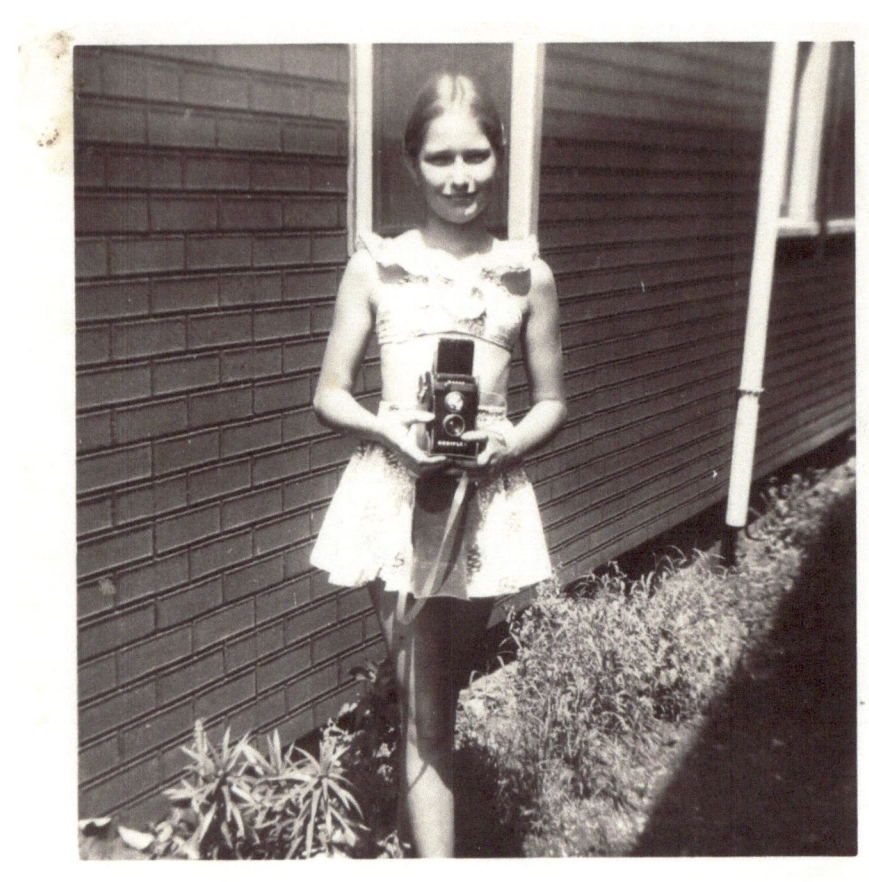

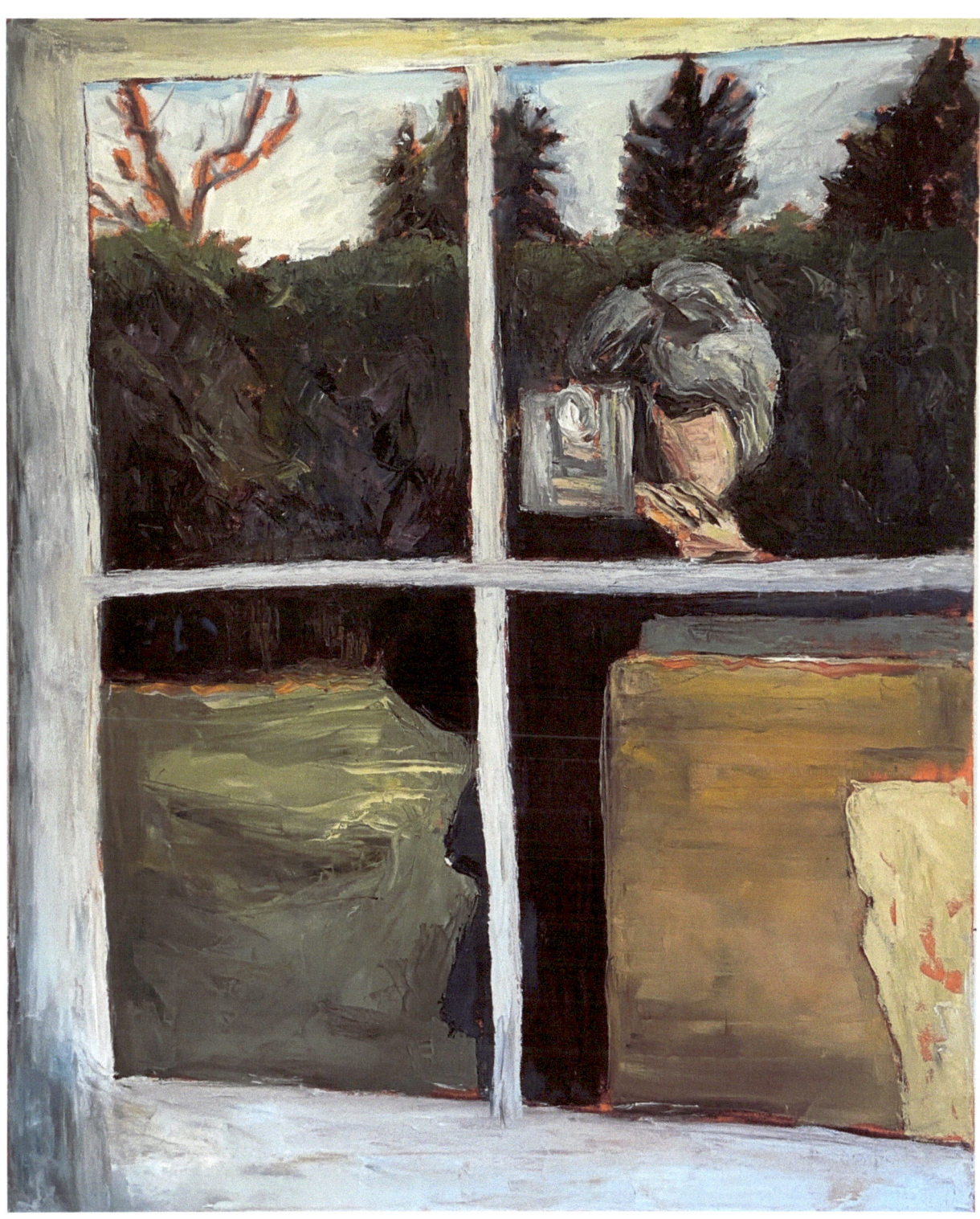

"Through the Window"

Grandma's House

Colorful, lively.

Decorated with red brocade drapes that fell to the floor.

Persian rugs, red Serouk with an overall pattern.

A tin ceiling, painted white.

Southeast facing.

Sun fell through the windows from both sides of the living room.

Spaghetti dinners for the workers helping her sons fight insurance companies gouging the poor.

Boston Baked Beans.

Holidays – Christmas and Jewish.

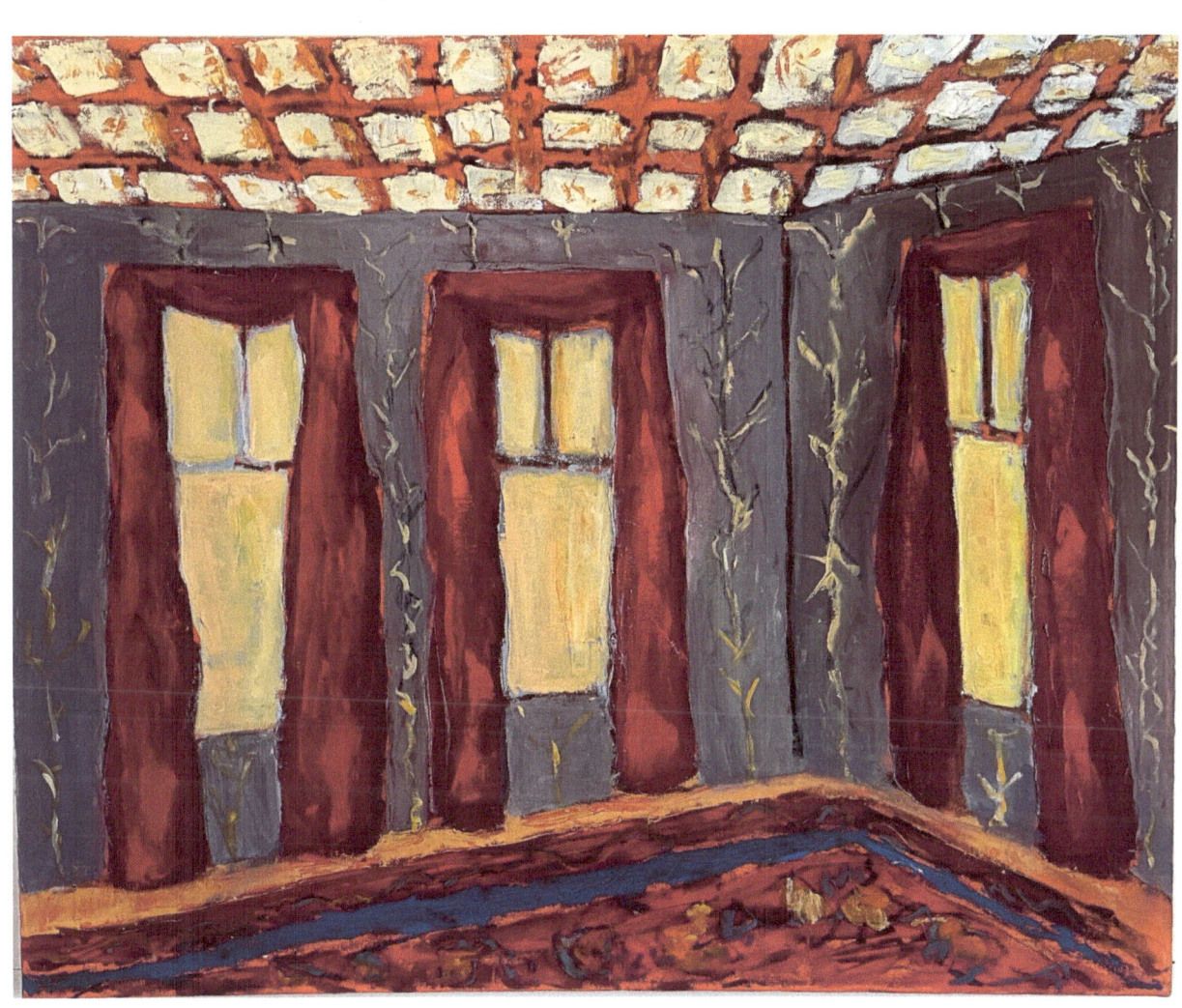

"Grandmother's Parlor"

Mother Rose – Grandma or Mother?
Happy to see me.
Her little debutante.
Just like the girls she'd seen on Beacon Hill.
I looked like them. Not Jewish?
Irish.
Like her husband, Bill, who had died suddenly.

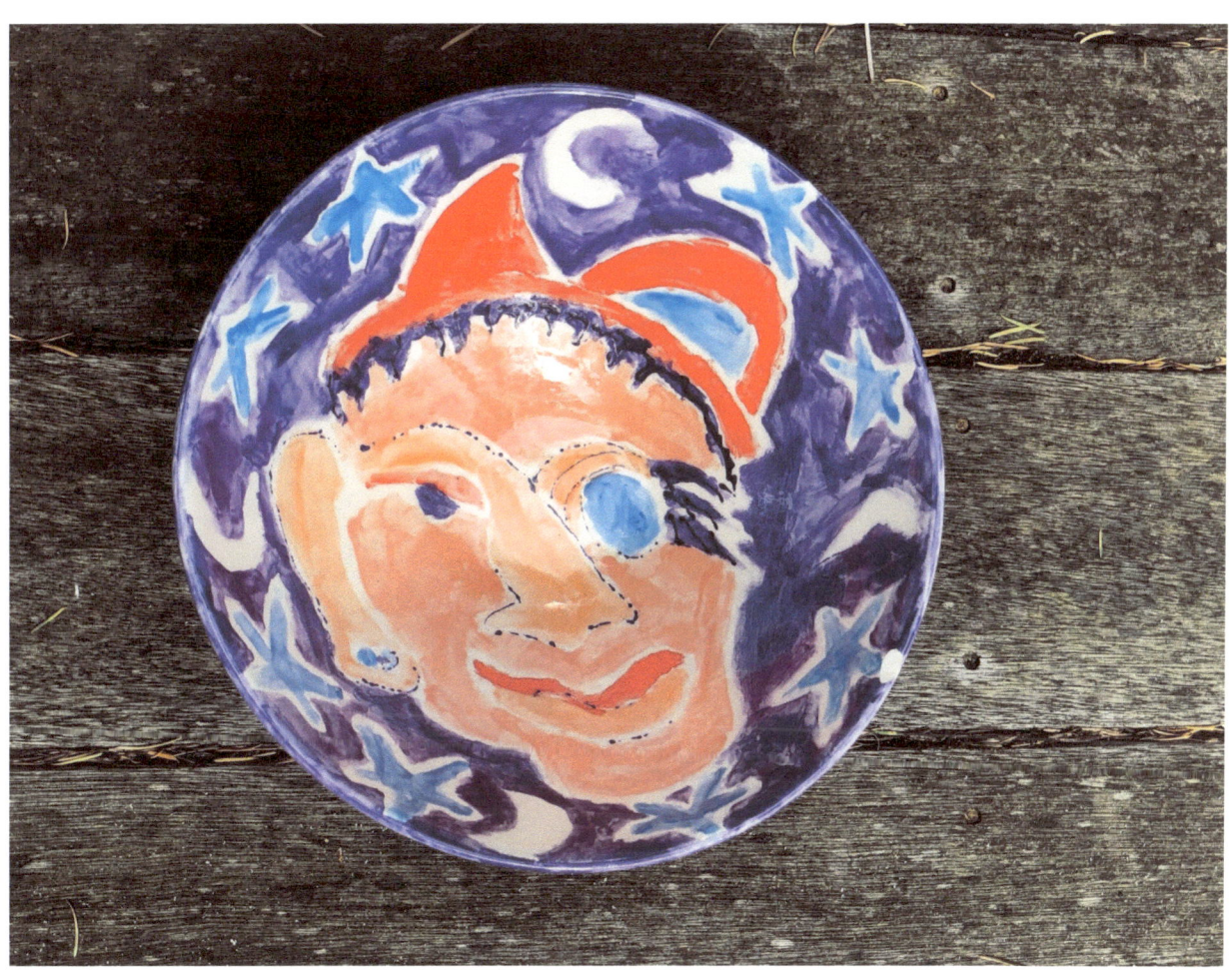

"Fairy Godmother Bowl"

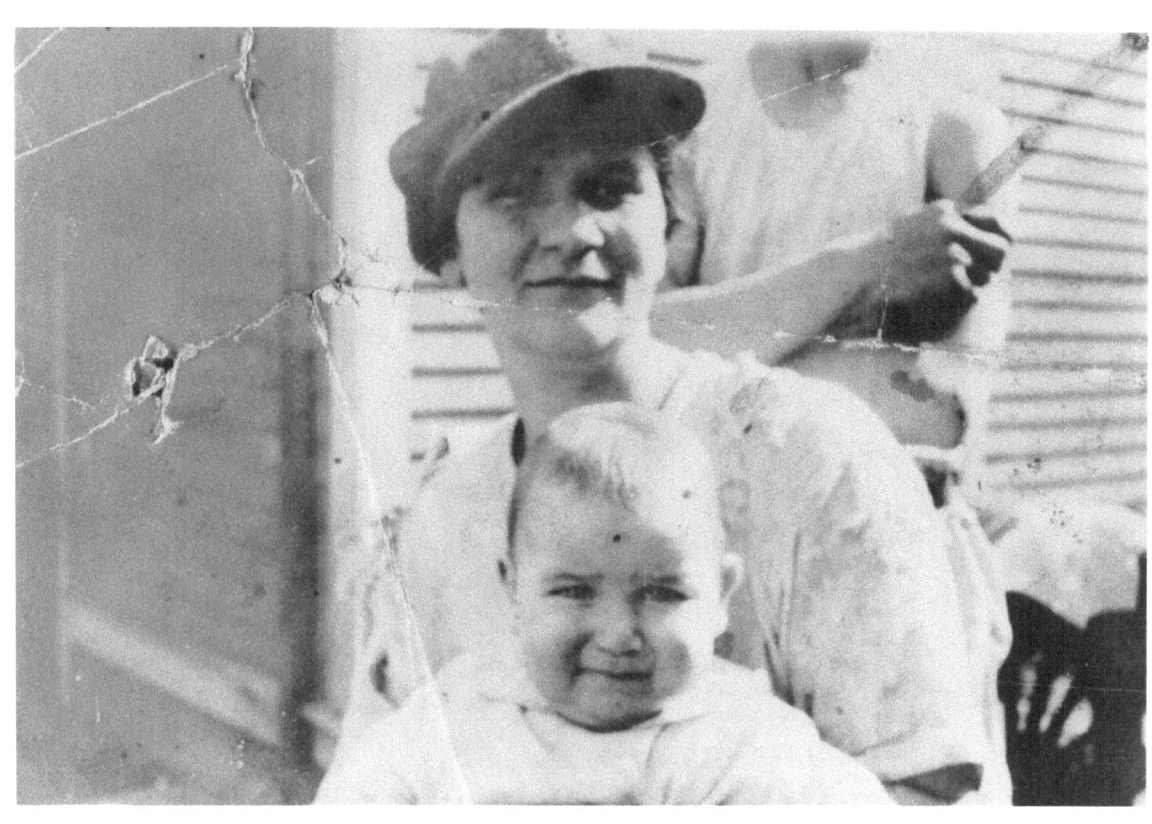

Home

We moved to the house next door when I was two-and-a-half.
Three months before my sister was born.

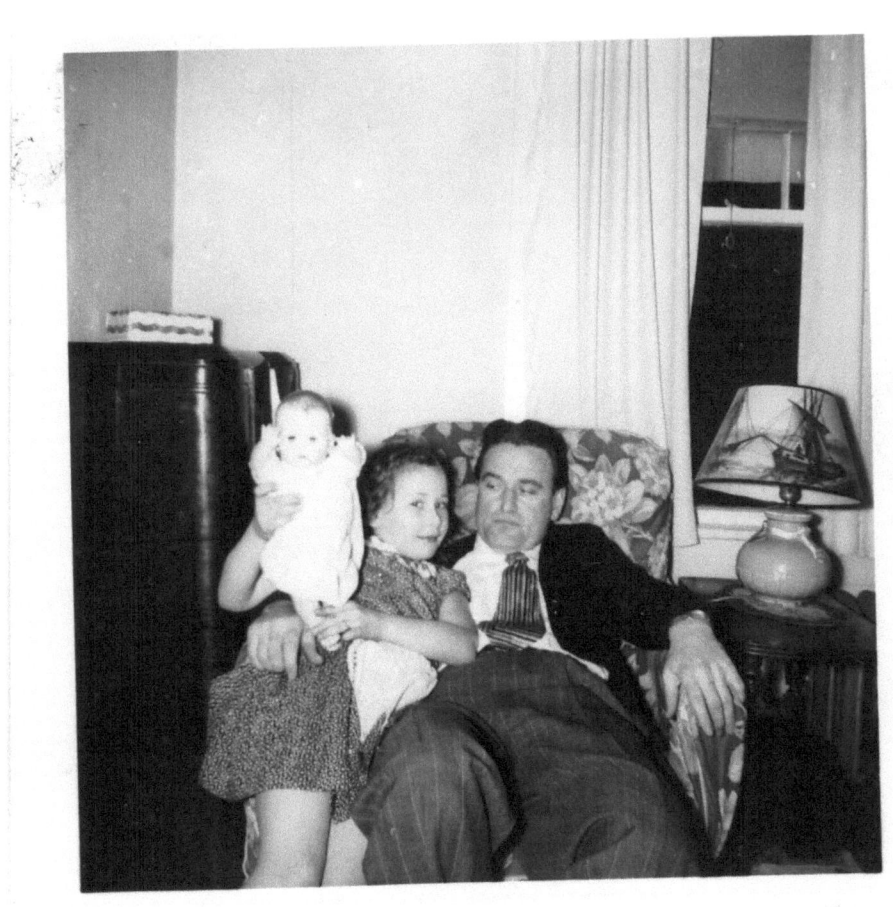

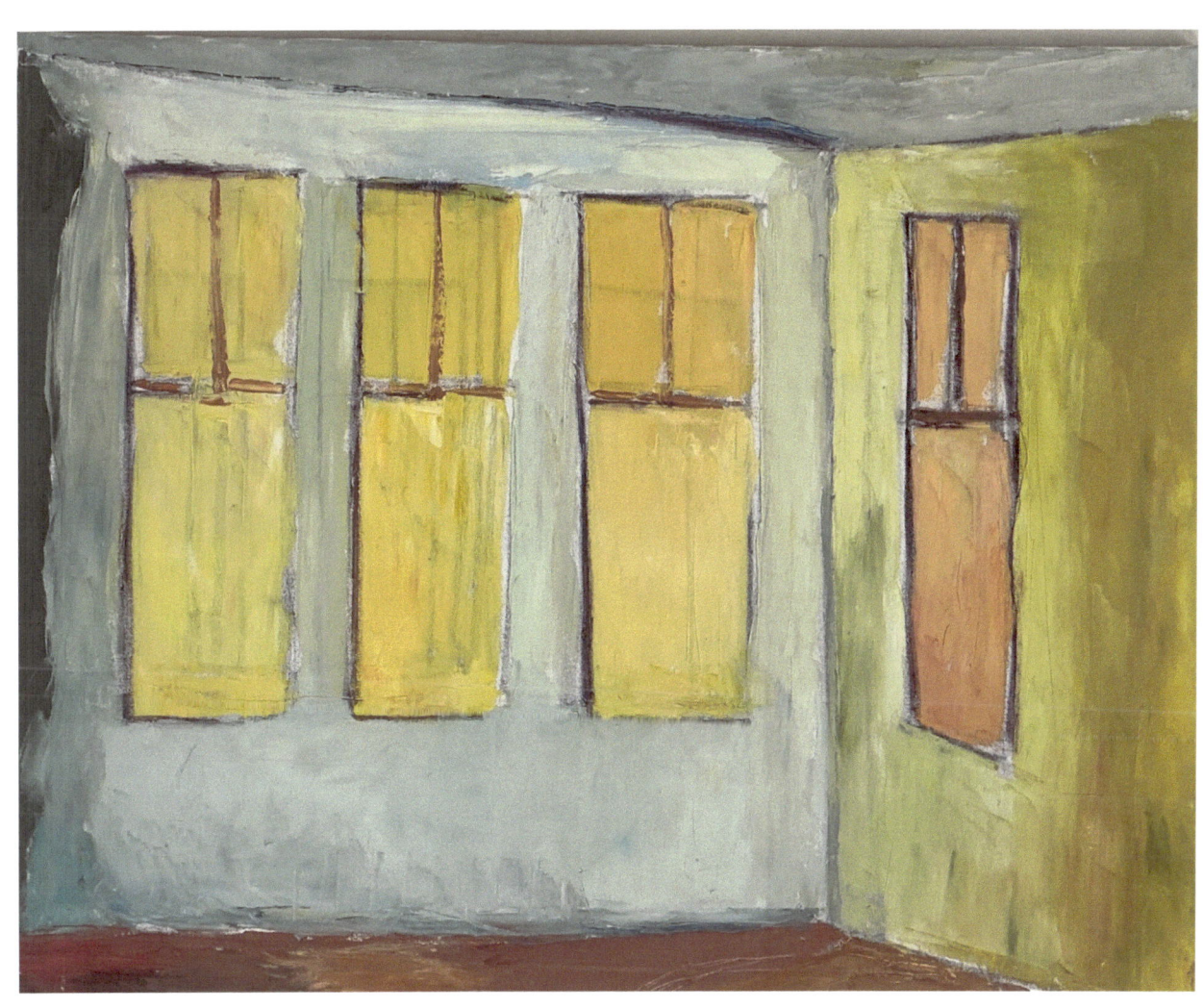

"Sunroom - My House"

The house was small, plain, and dark.
Dark green, maroon furniture and rugs.
My father was a lawyer
and worked the nightshift at the post office.
Happy in the morning, reciting poetry.
Remote in the evening, home from work.
He watched TV, slept on the couch.

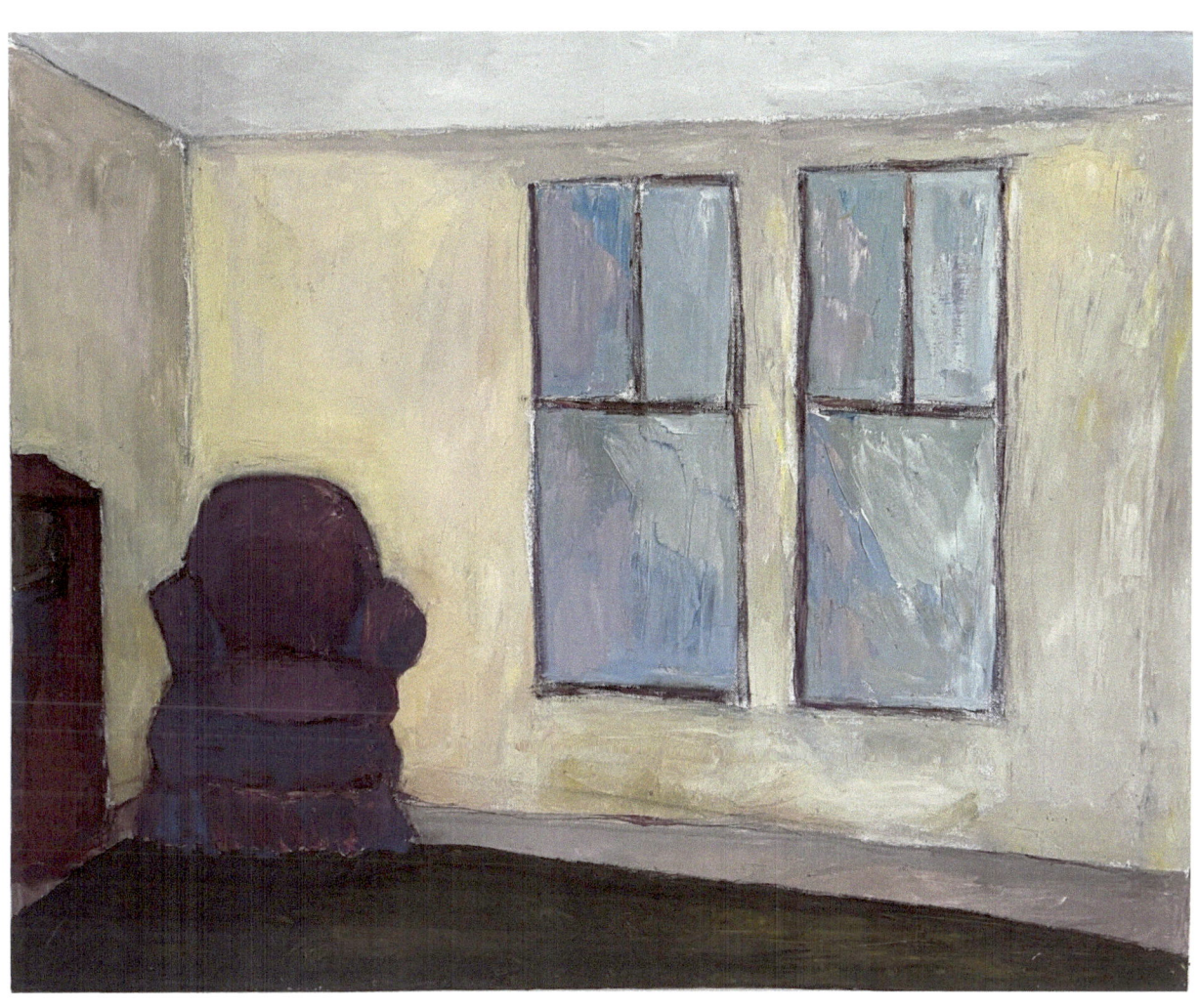

"My Father's Chair"

He put me on trial.
"Your points are irrelevant and immaterial."

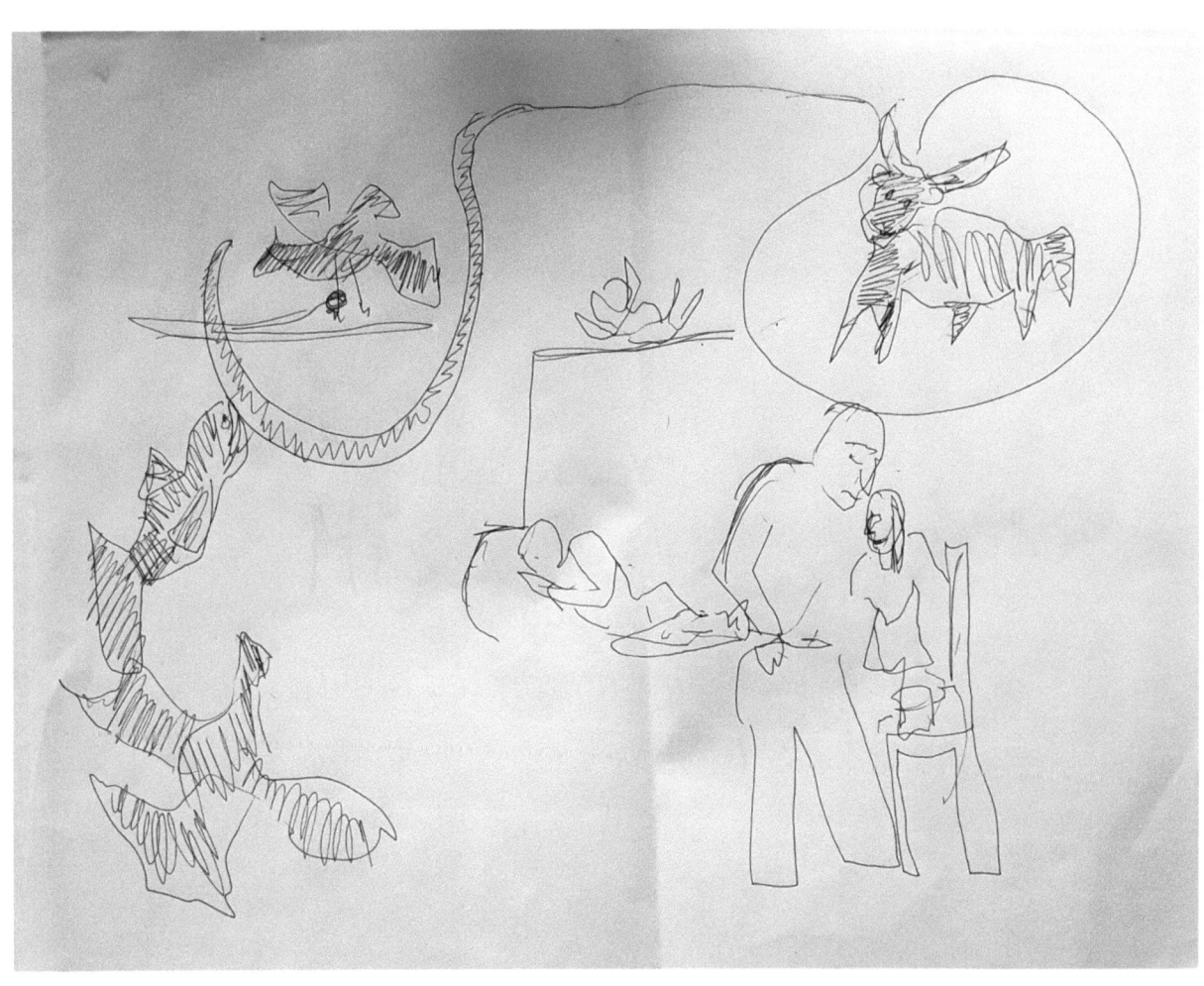

"The Father I Wish I Had"

"You're Spoiled!"

She was the mother.
She made the rules.
She interpreted reality.

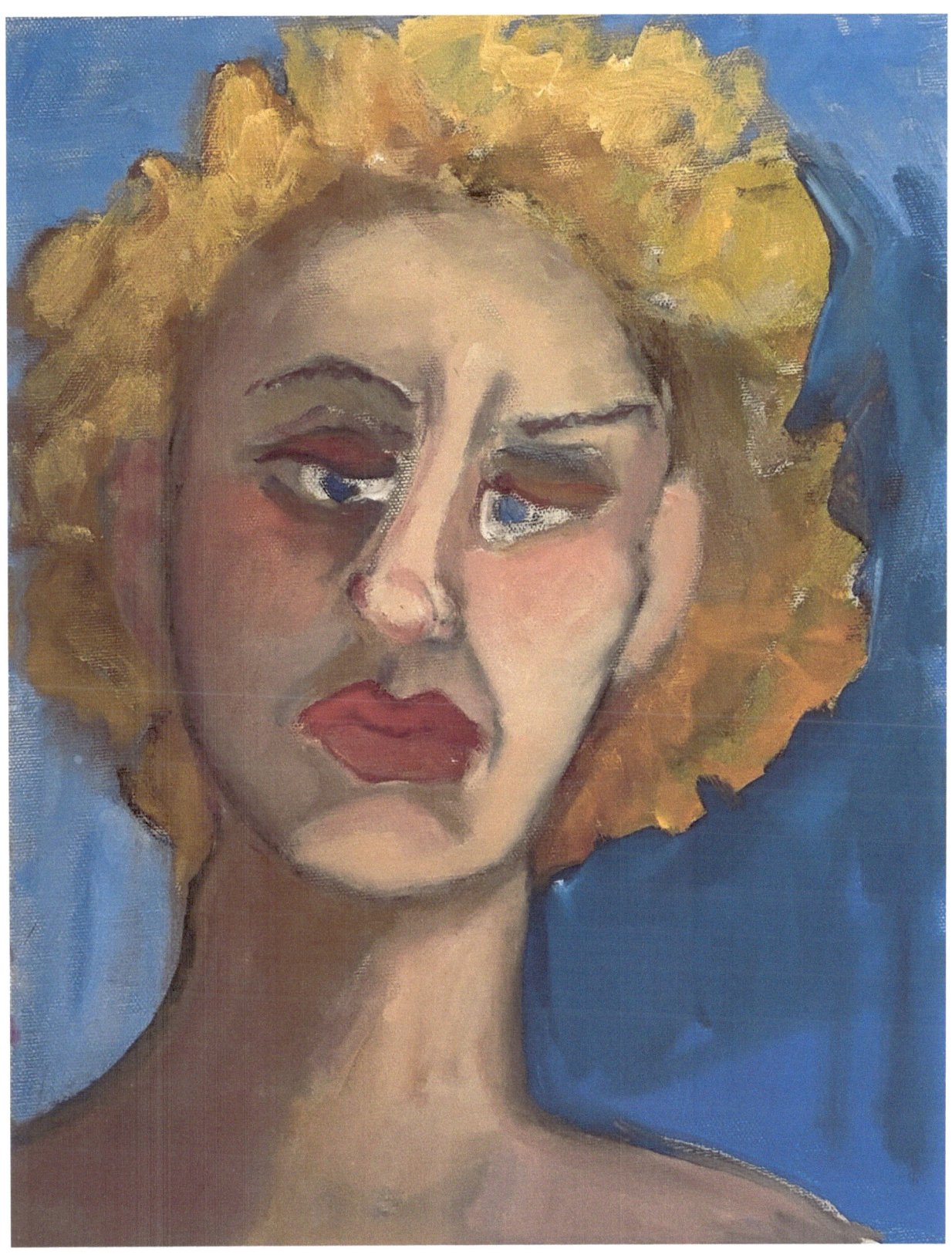

"Mother #1"

My mother's perceptions and judgements were off-kilter.
She was depressed and anxious.
She never learned to drive.
She had the power of the purse.

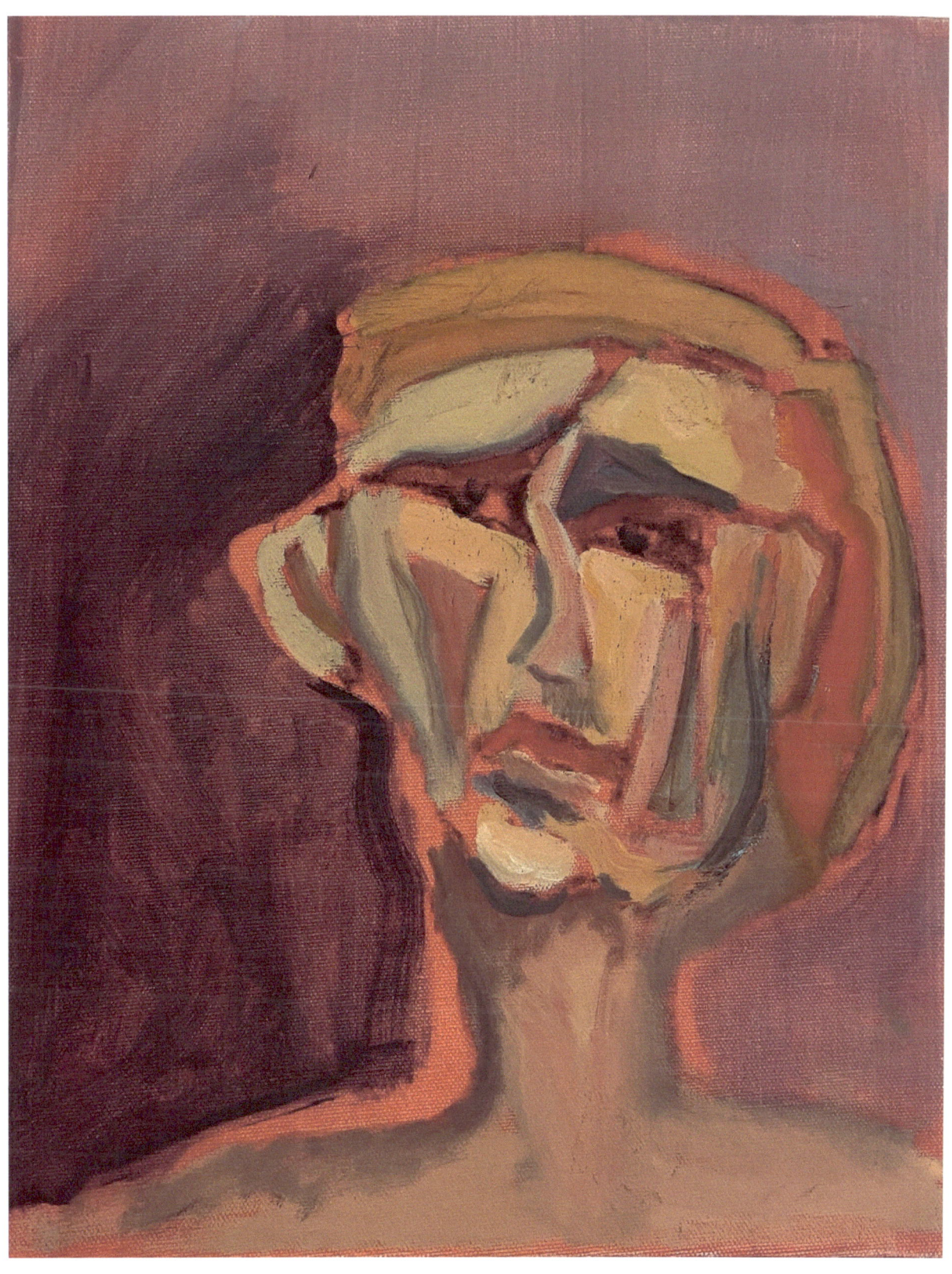

"Mother #2"

And viciously attacked me and my father.
He had to convince her to give him the money for a new car.
Life doesn't have to be like this.

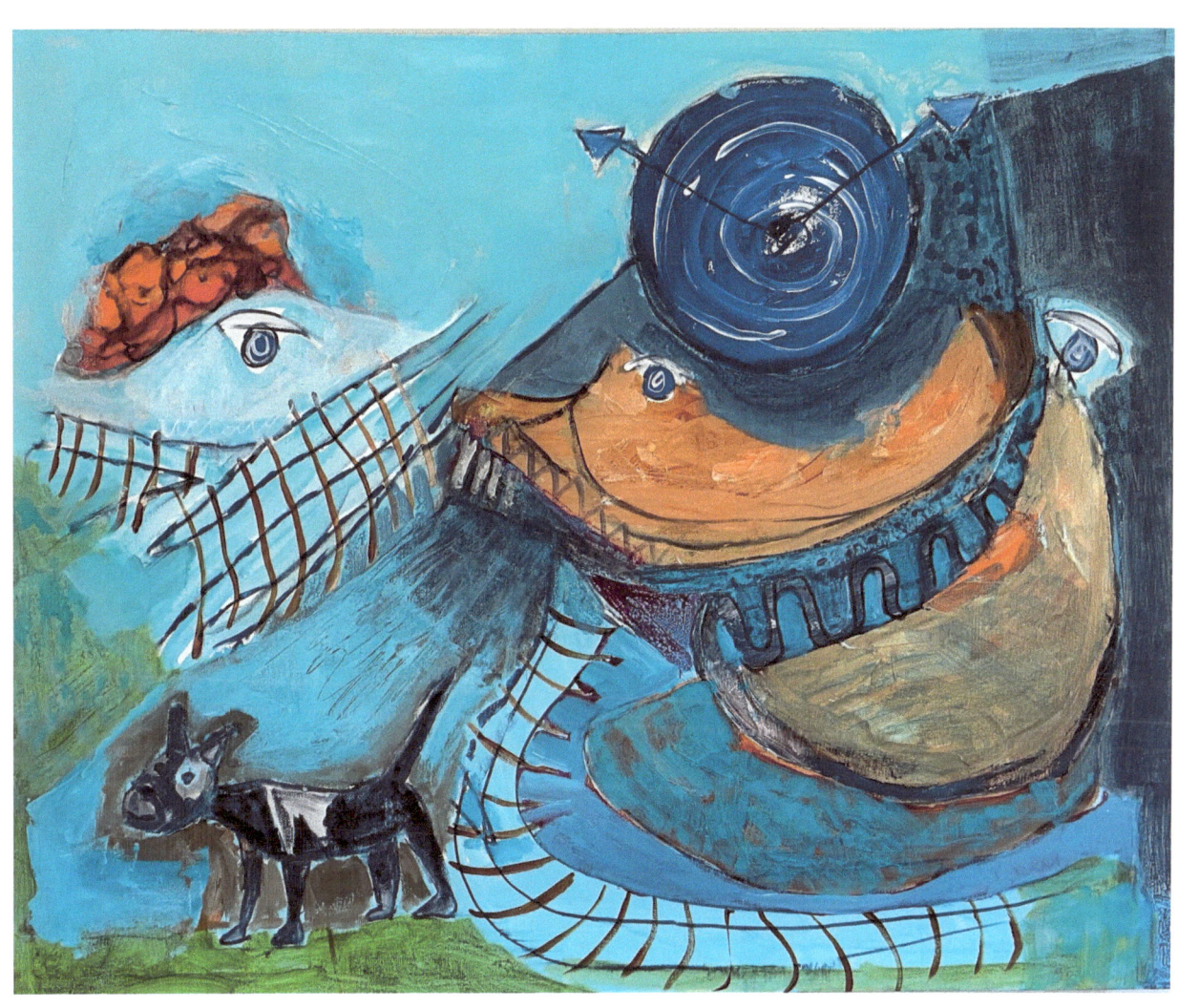

"Clash / Crash"

Portrait of my Mother

She had a difficult childhood.
Caught in Russia/Poland during World War I
with her mother, aunt, and her brother and sister.
Her father had gone ahead to the U.S.,
to earn money to bring the family over.

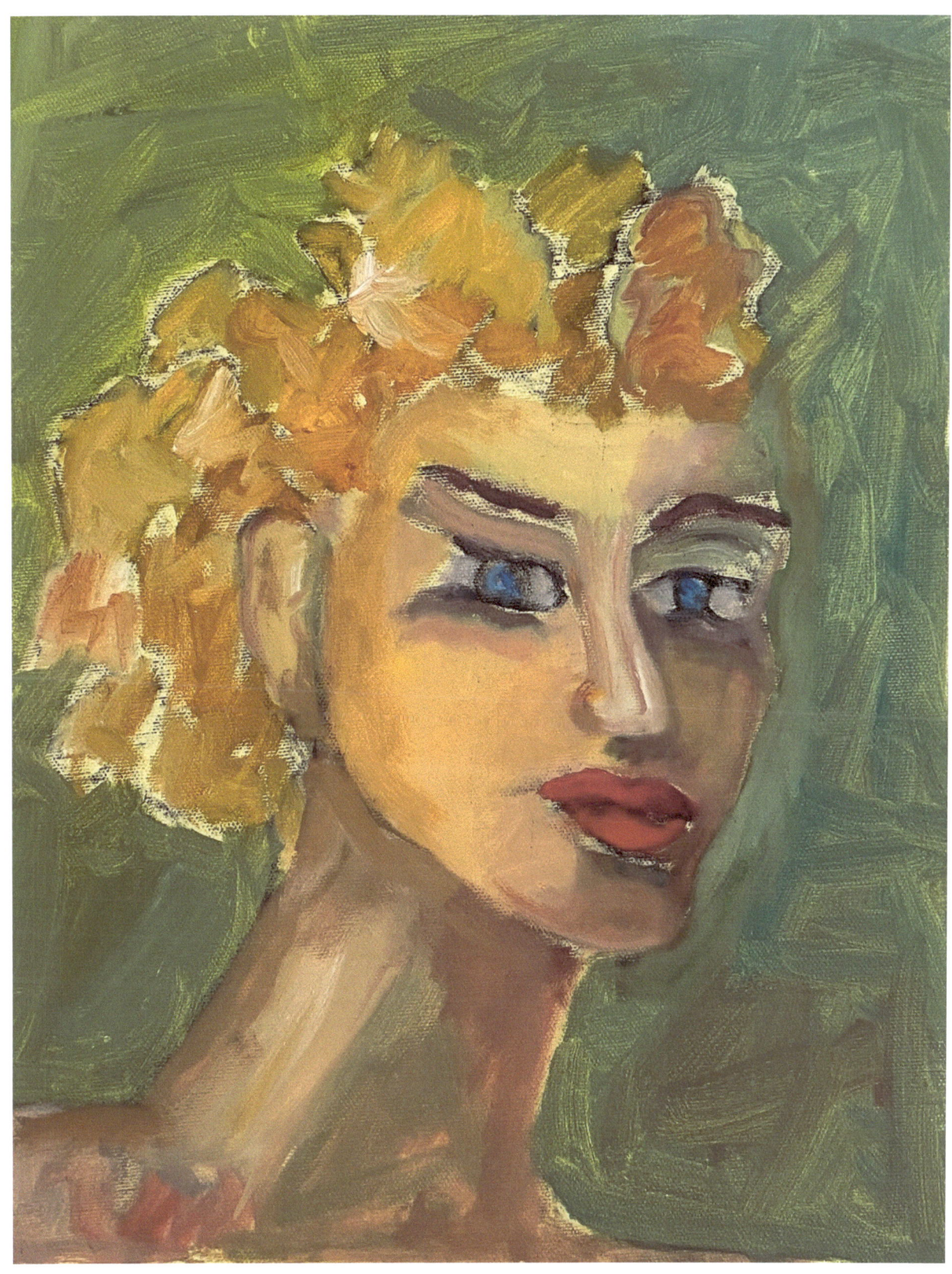

"Mother #3"

*"My father didn't make enough money
to send me to college," she said.
Two weeks before I entered college,
she decided not to take my tuition money
out of her bank account.*

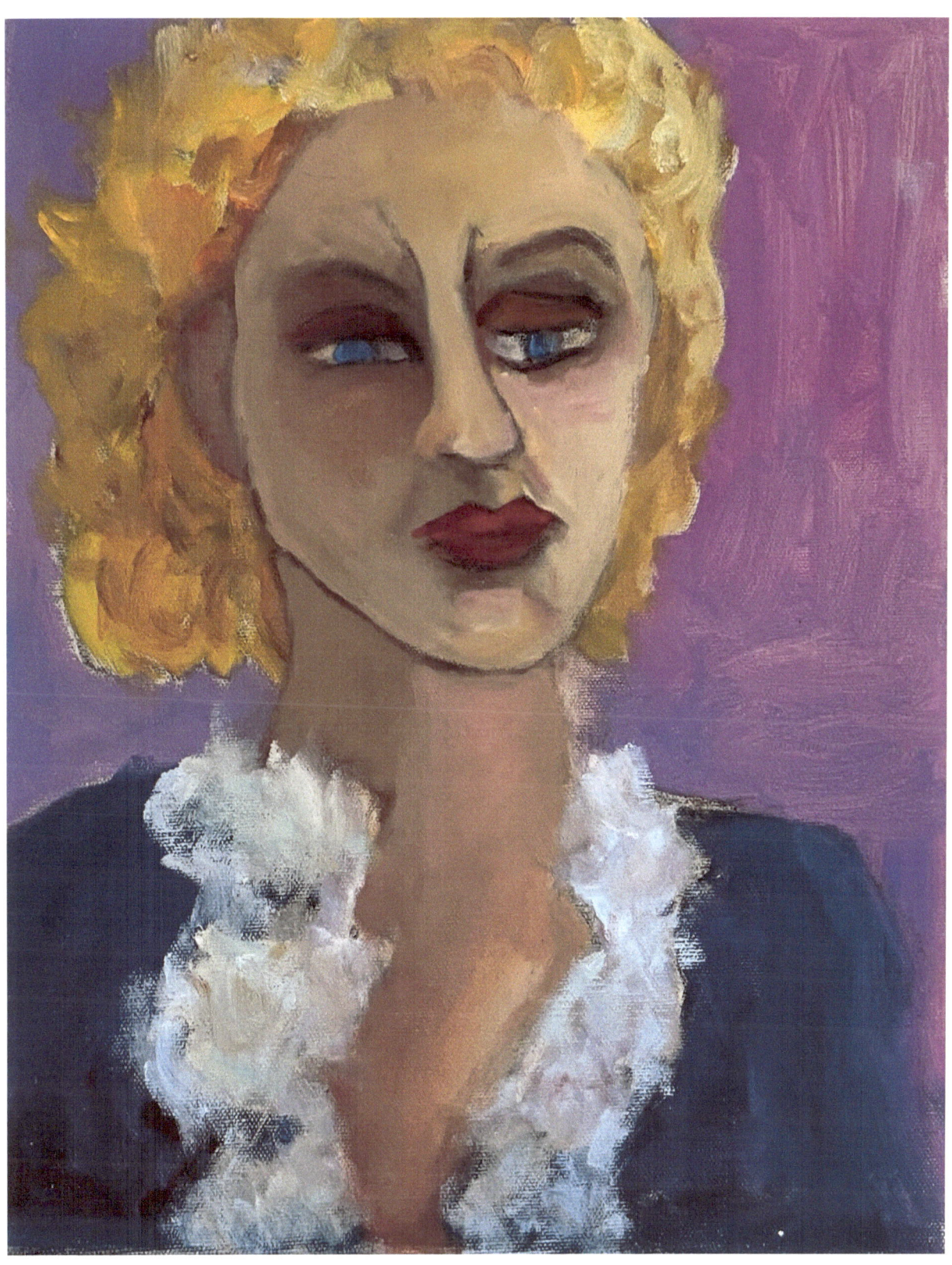

"Mother #4"

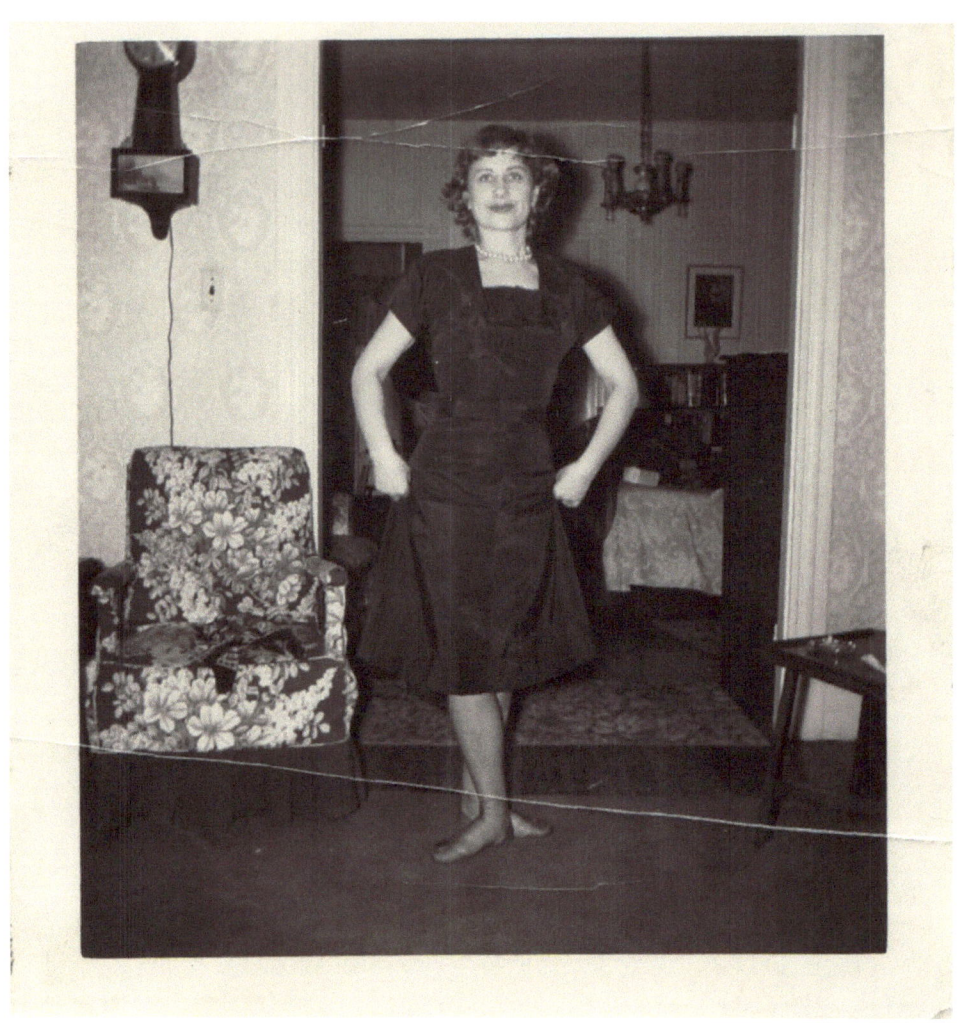

"Try and make me! You're not my boss!"
It cost too much, she said, to develop my photos.
She took my Ansco camera away.

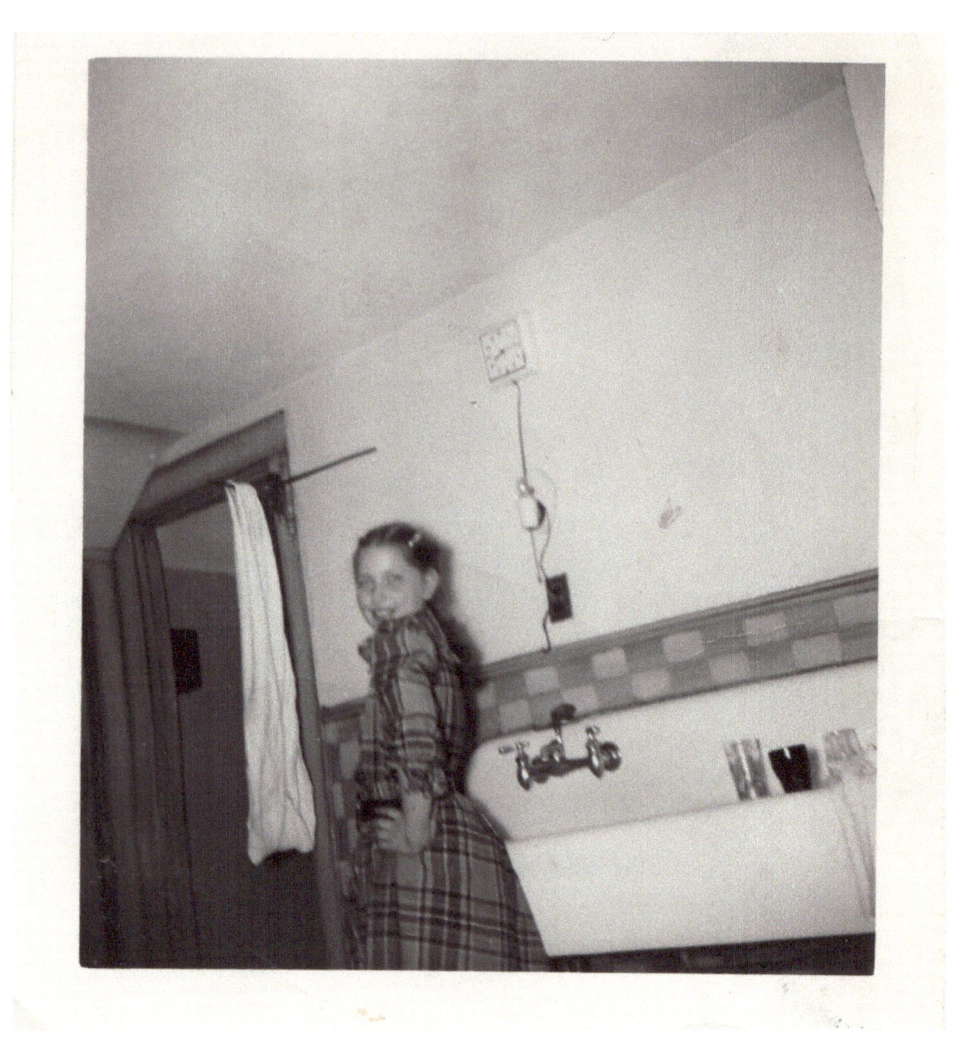

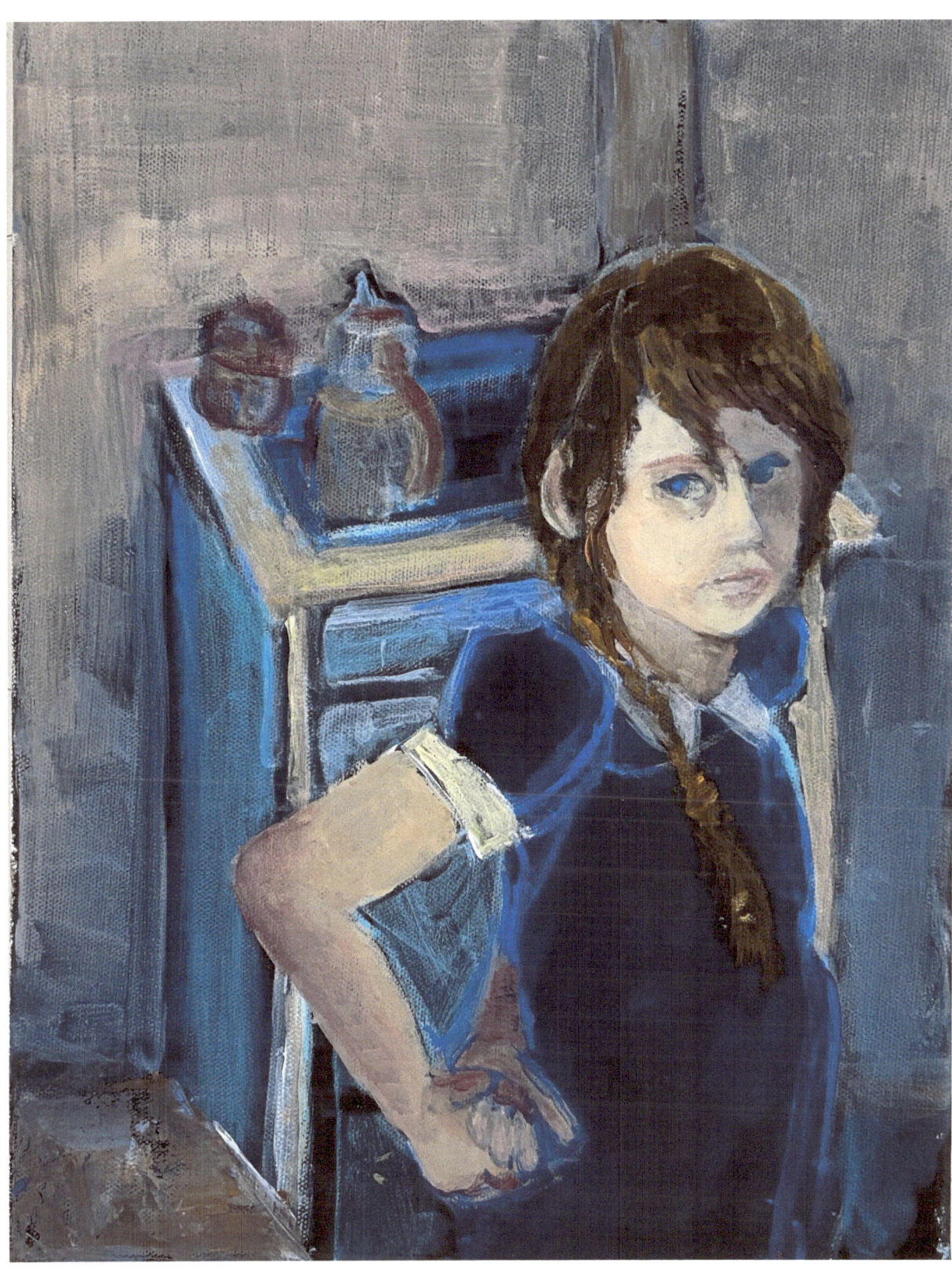

"Try and Make Me!"

Family Portrait

Mother is a cat. Dressed to the nines, self-absorbed.
Father is a goat. Absent, unavailable.
Sister is a doll. She was fun to be around. "Miss Personality."
Me, I'm a dog. Ready to run. "I'm outta here!"

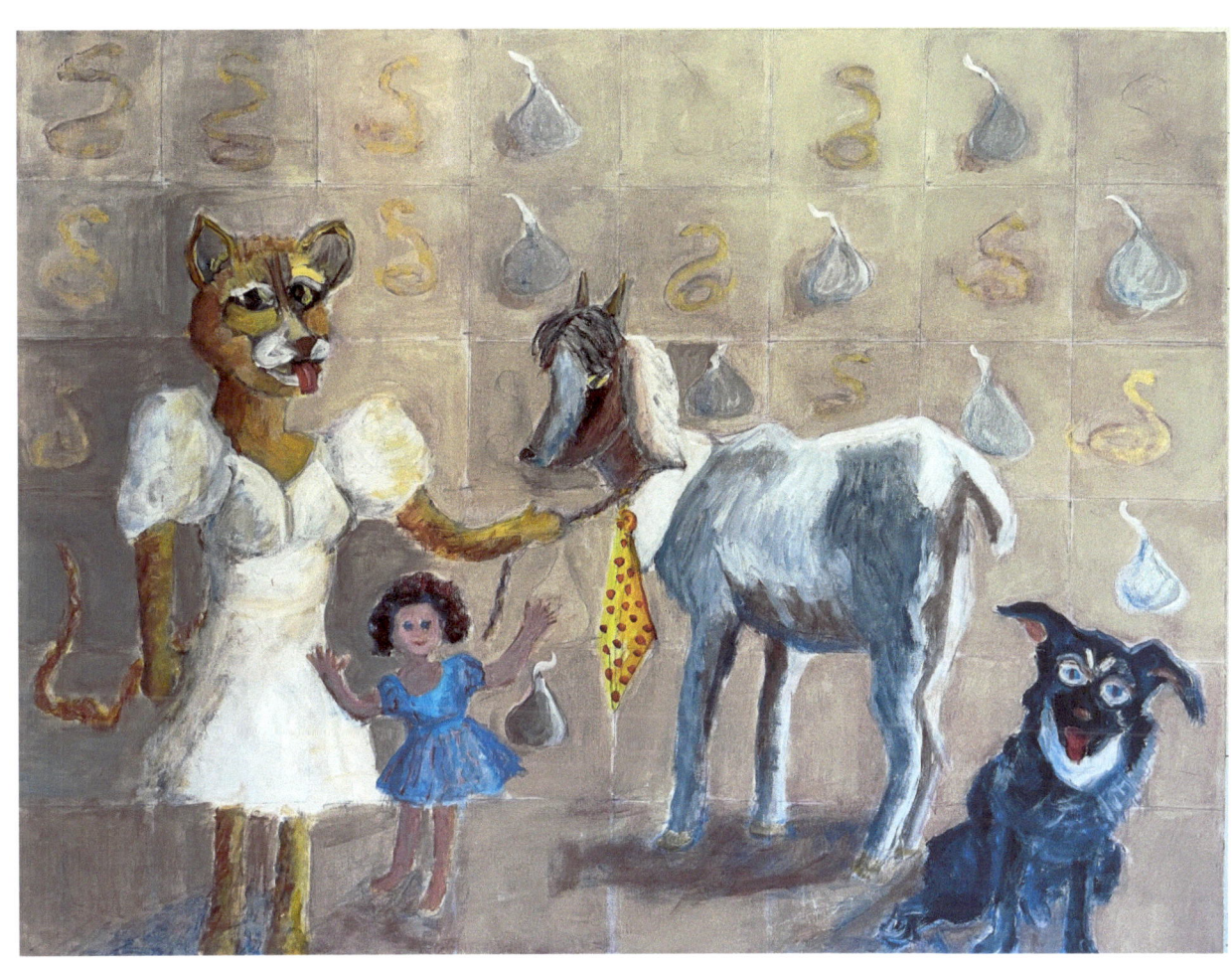

"Family Circus"

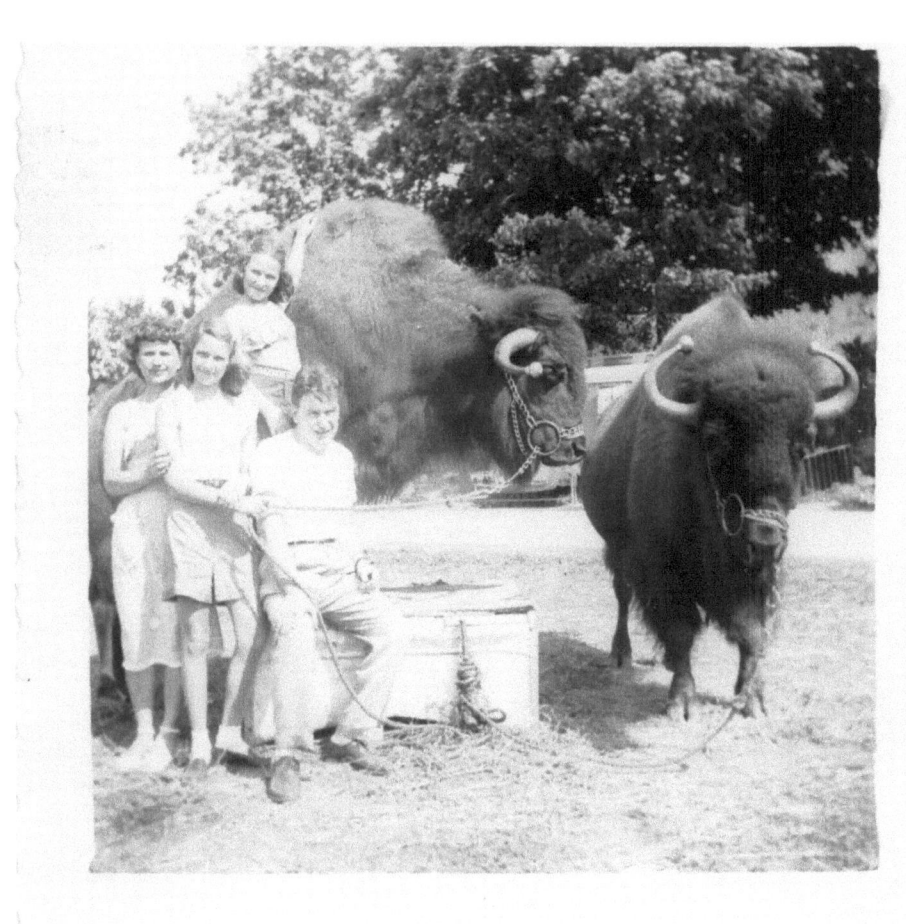

The Big Alone

As I matured, I looked great on the outside.

Inside, the emotions did not match.

Empty.

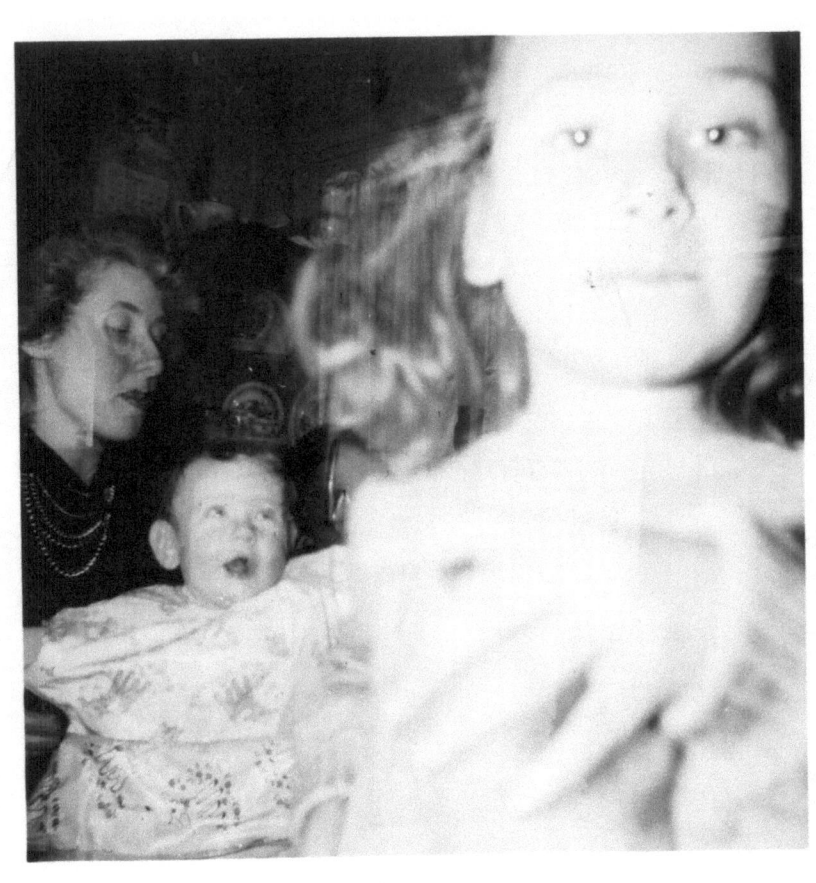

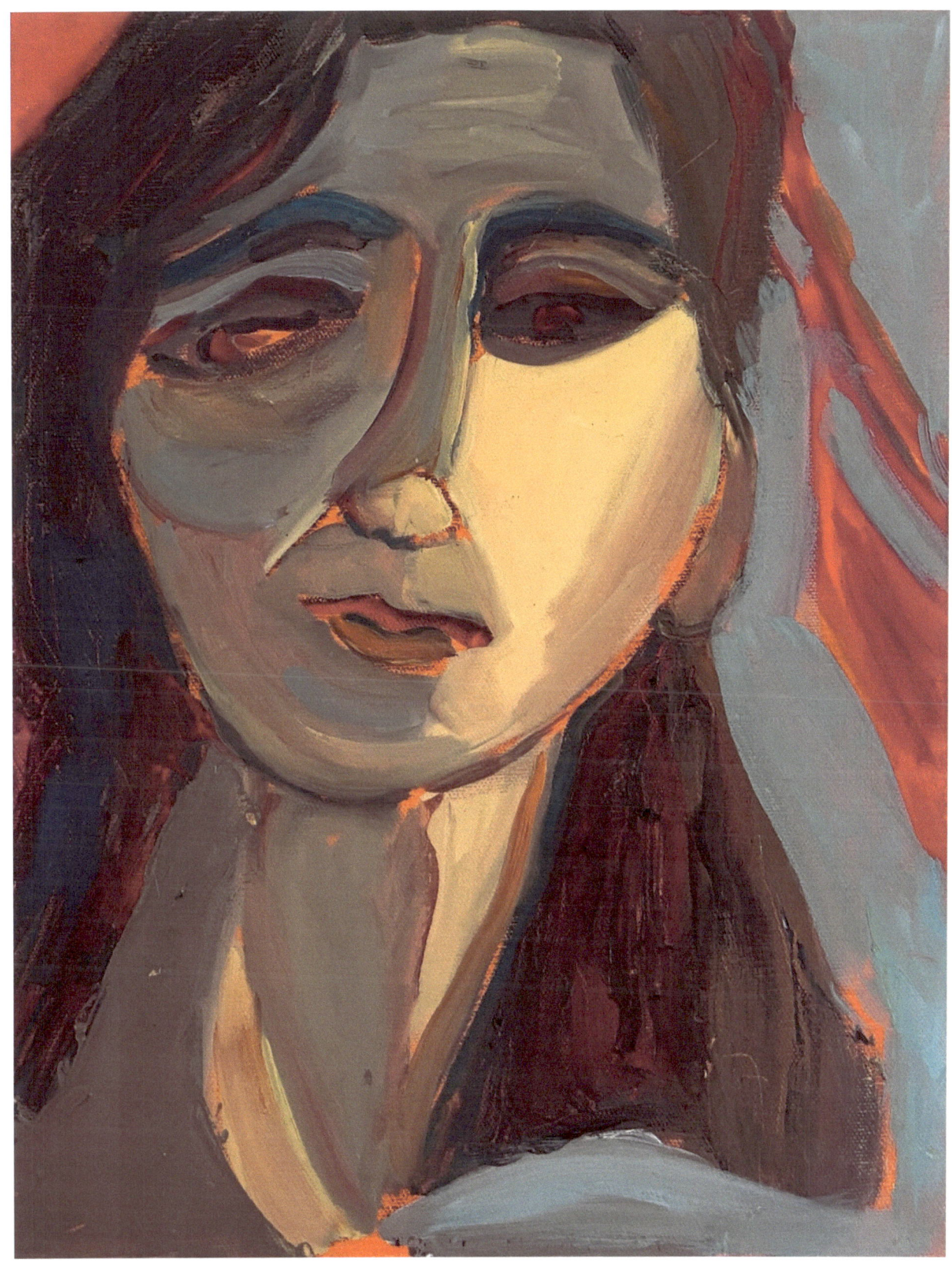

"Self-Portrait"

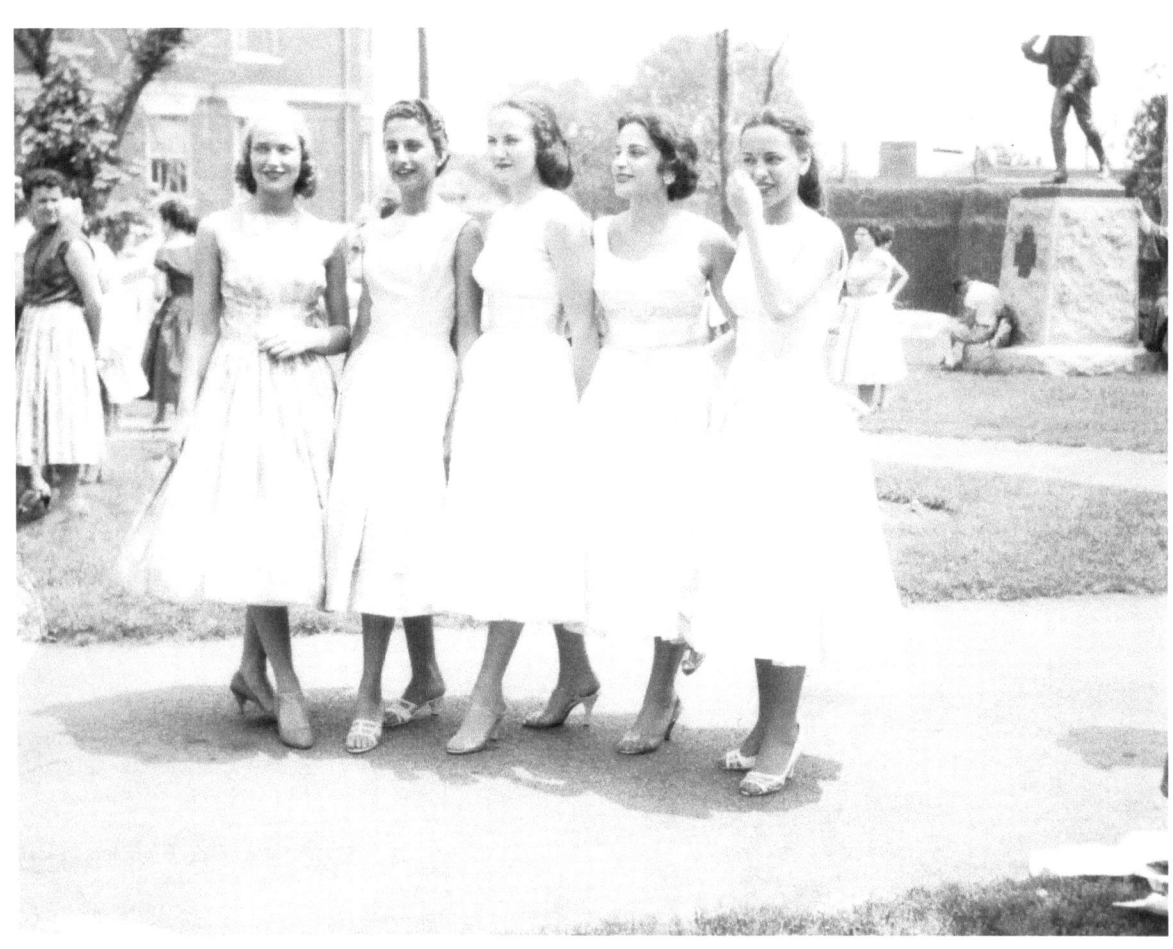

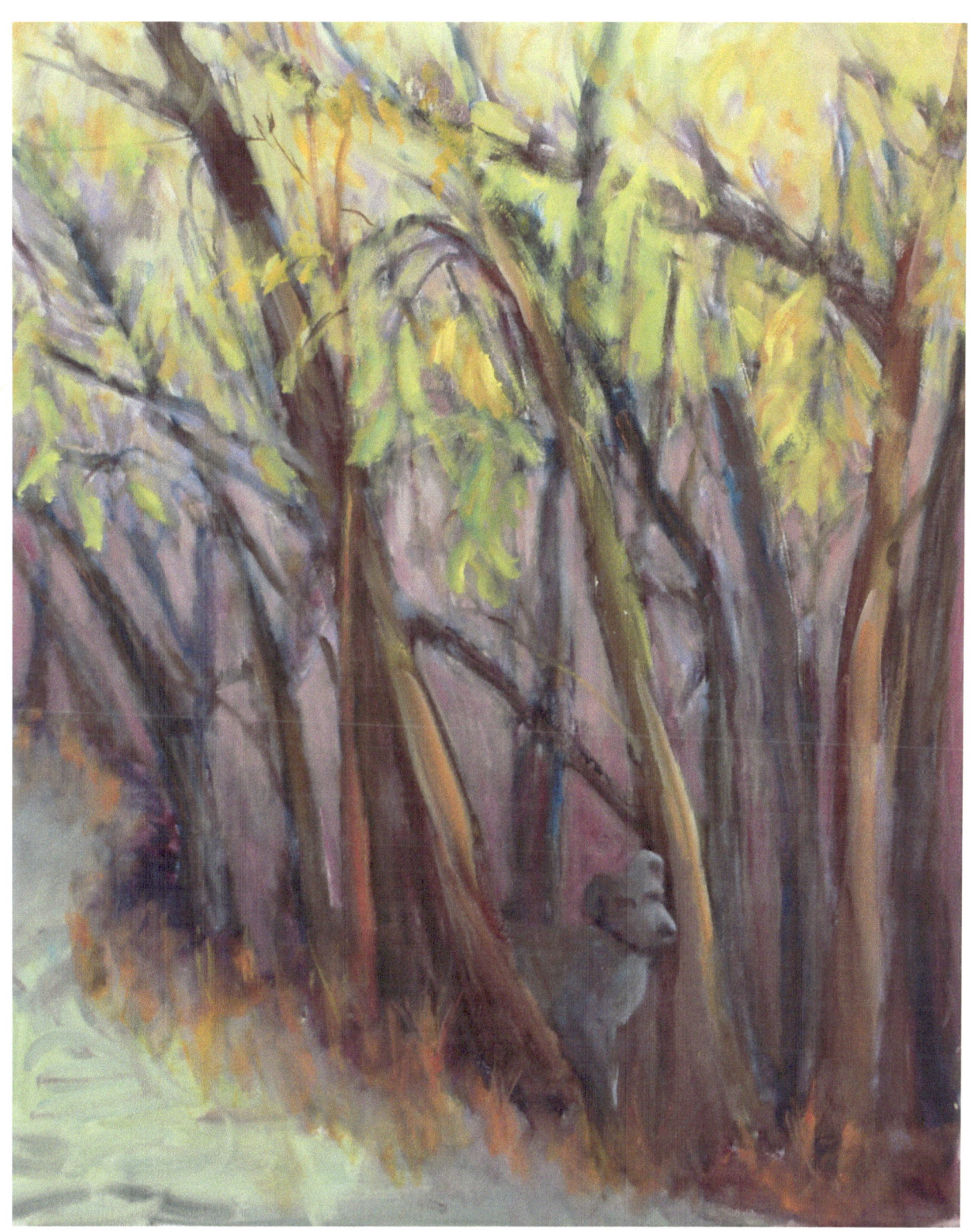

"Big Alone #1"

Love and Marriage

*Maybe having someone to love, who loved me,
would cure my self-doubt.*

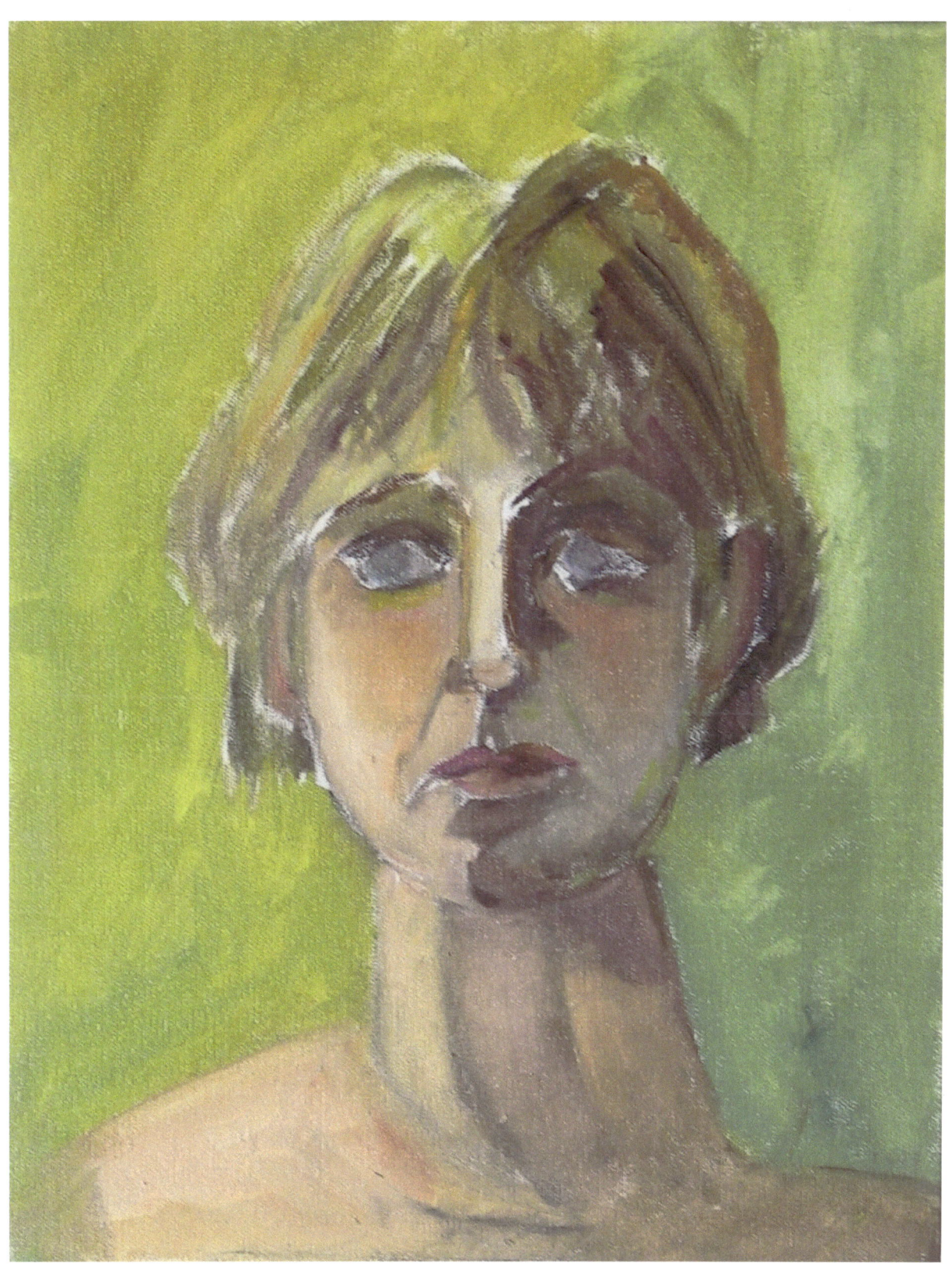

"Big Alone #2"

My romantic fantasy. David Maron.
The reality?
Two unhappy, disconnected people.
Bored.

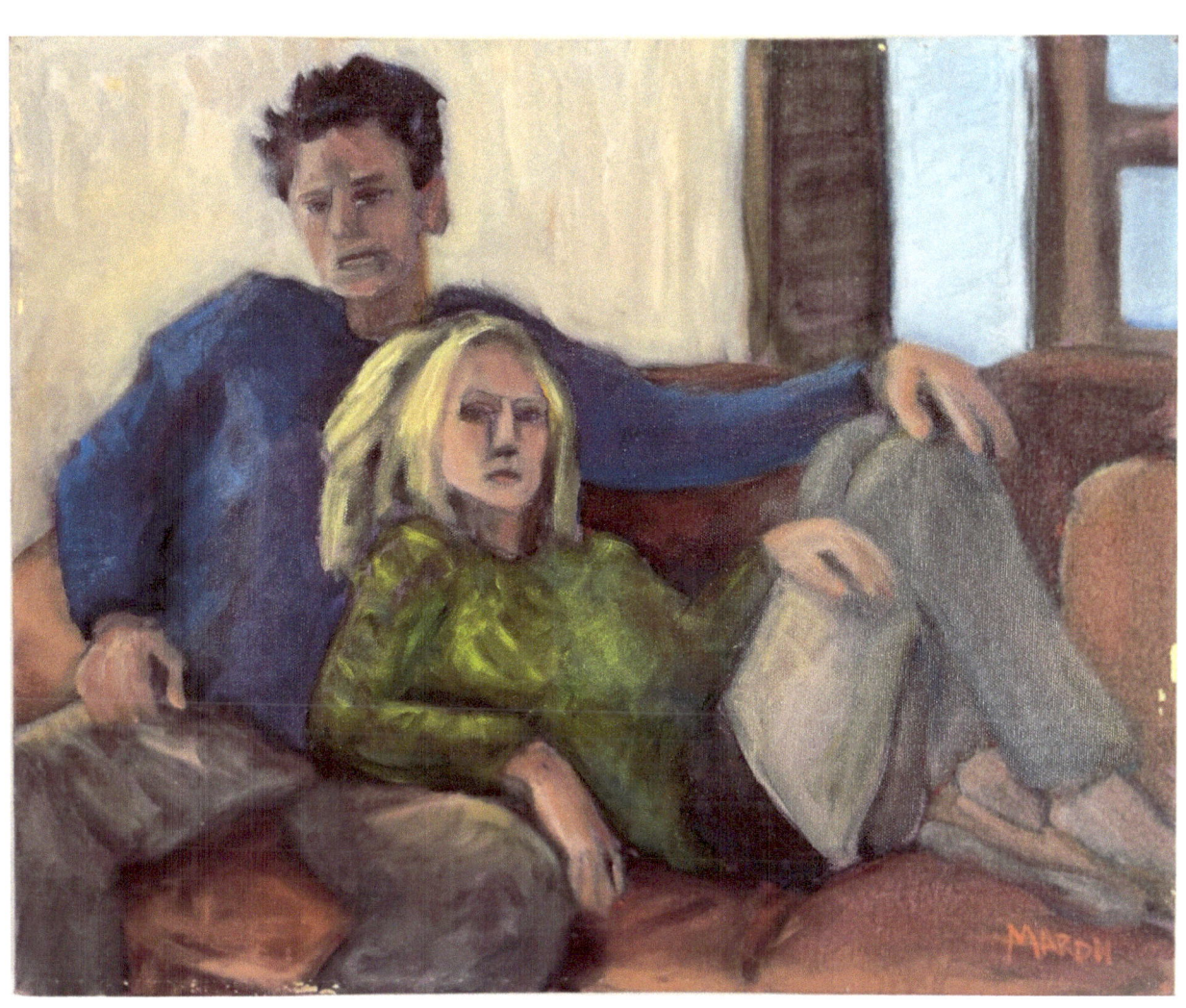

"Sunday Afternoon"

I had my first son, Bill, at 19.
Jonathan and Joel, mirror-image twins,
were born three years later.
I returned to Tufts at 24.
Divorced at 27.
Graduated from college at 28.

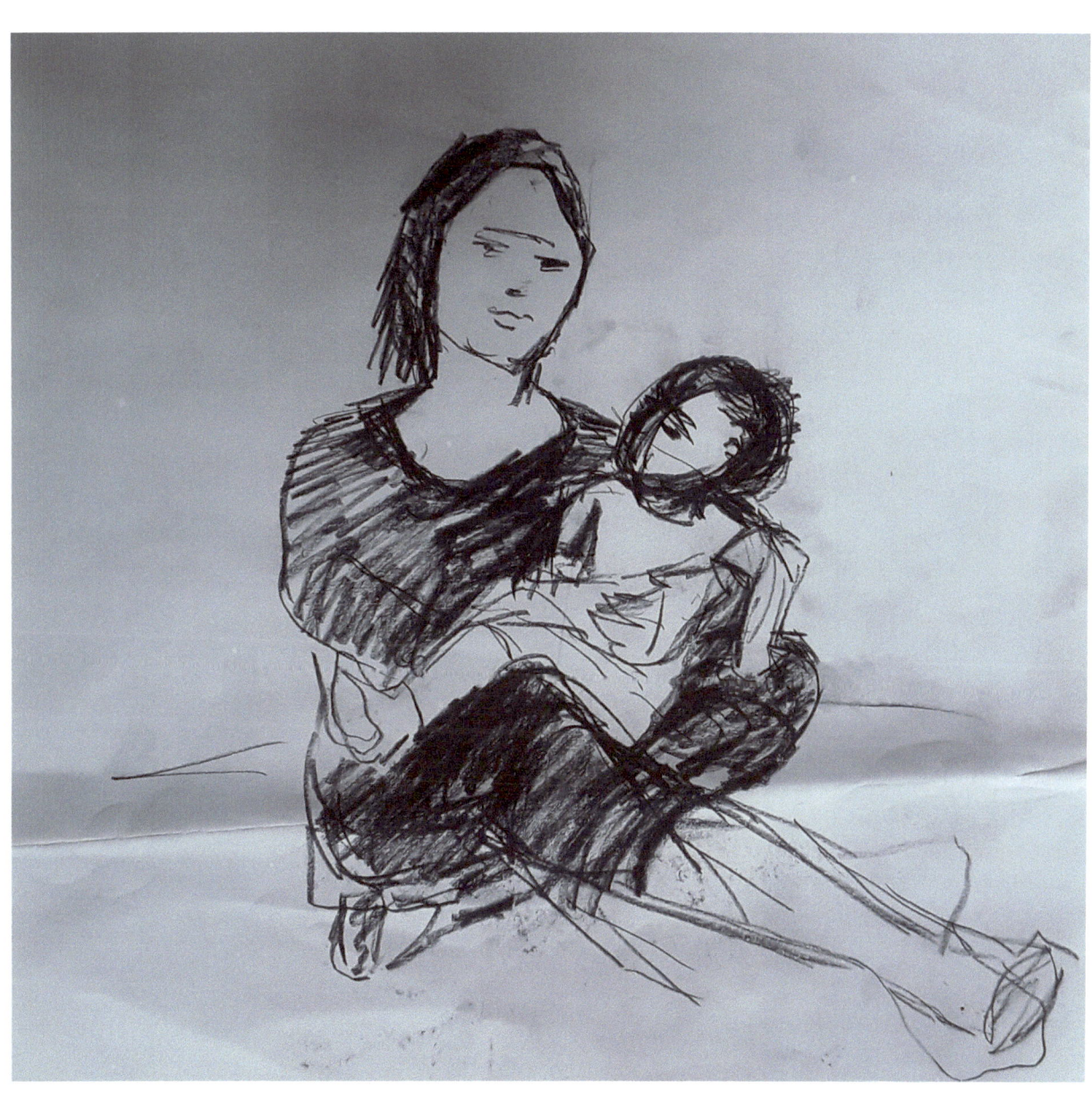

"Mother and Child"

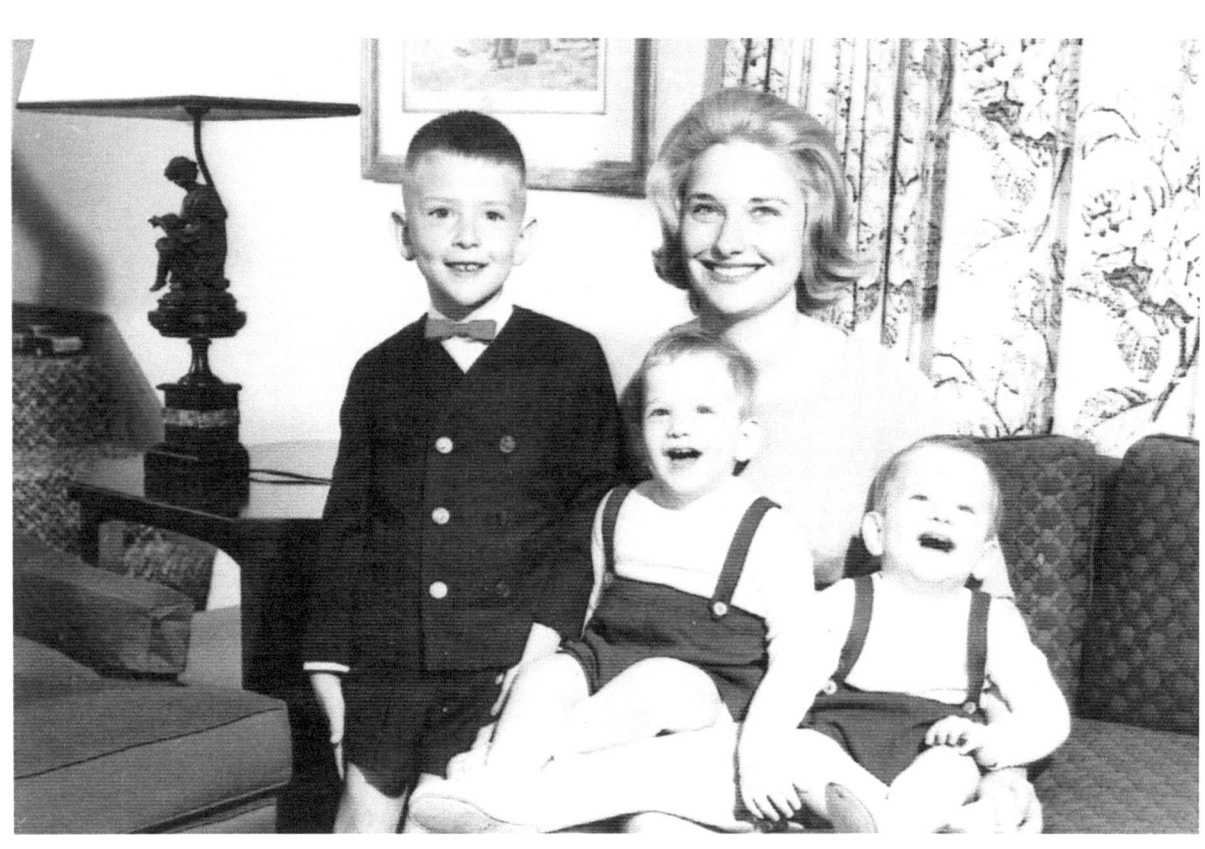

Me and My Creative Spirit

My alter ego.
The child who play-acted.
The girl who loved to take pictures with her Ansco
emerges again.

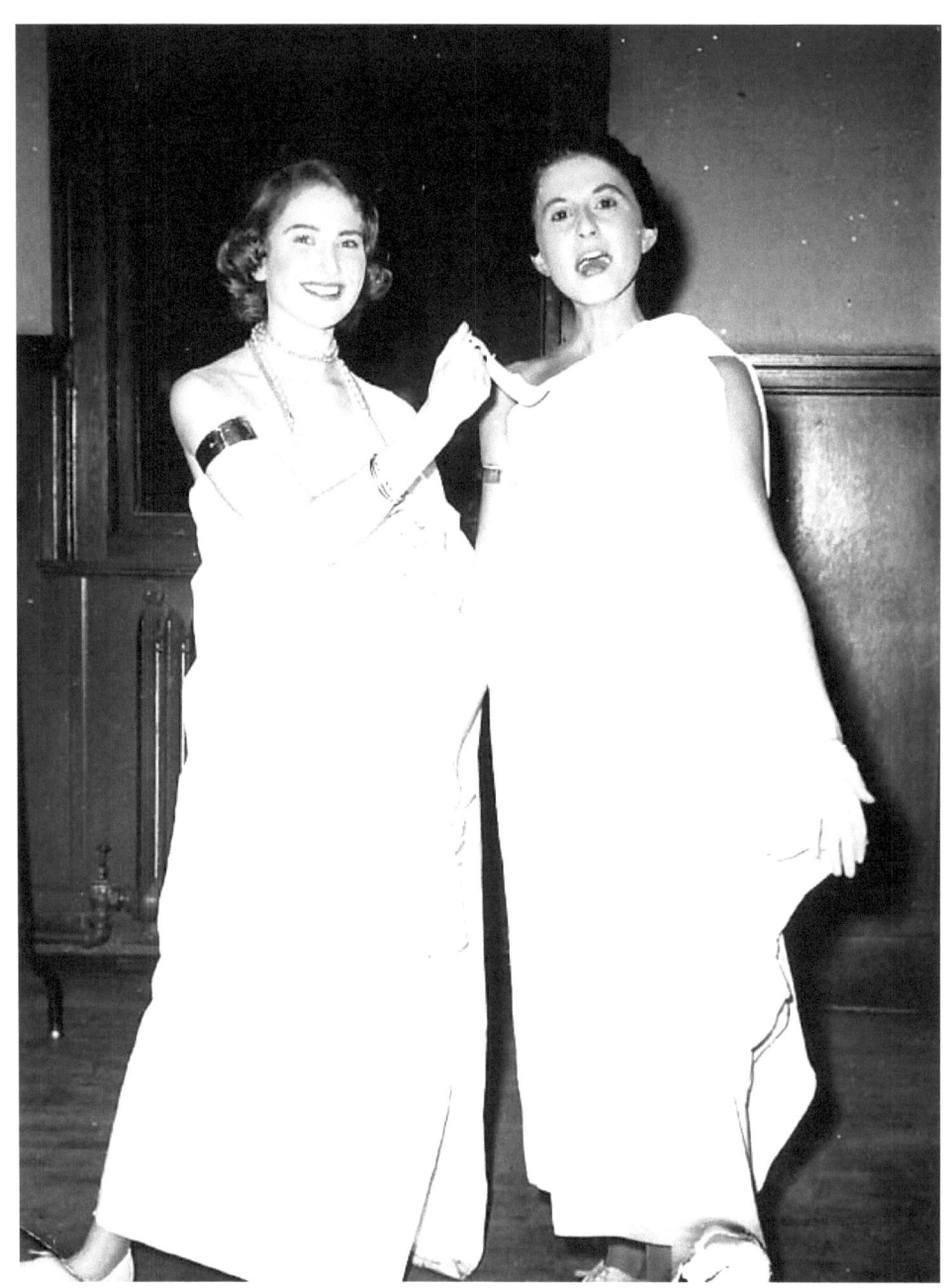

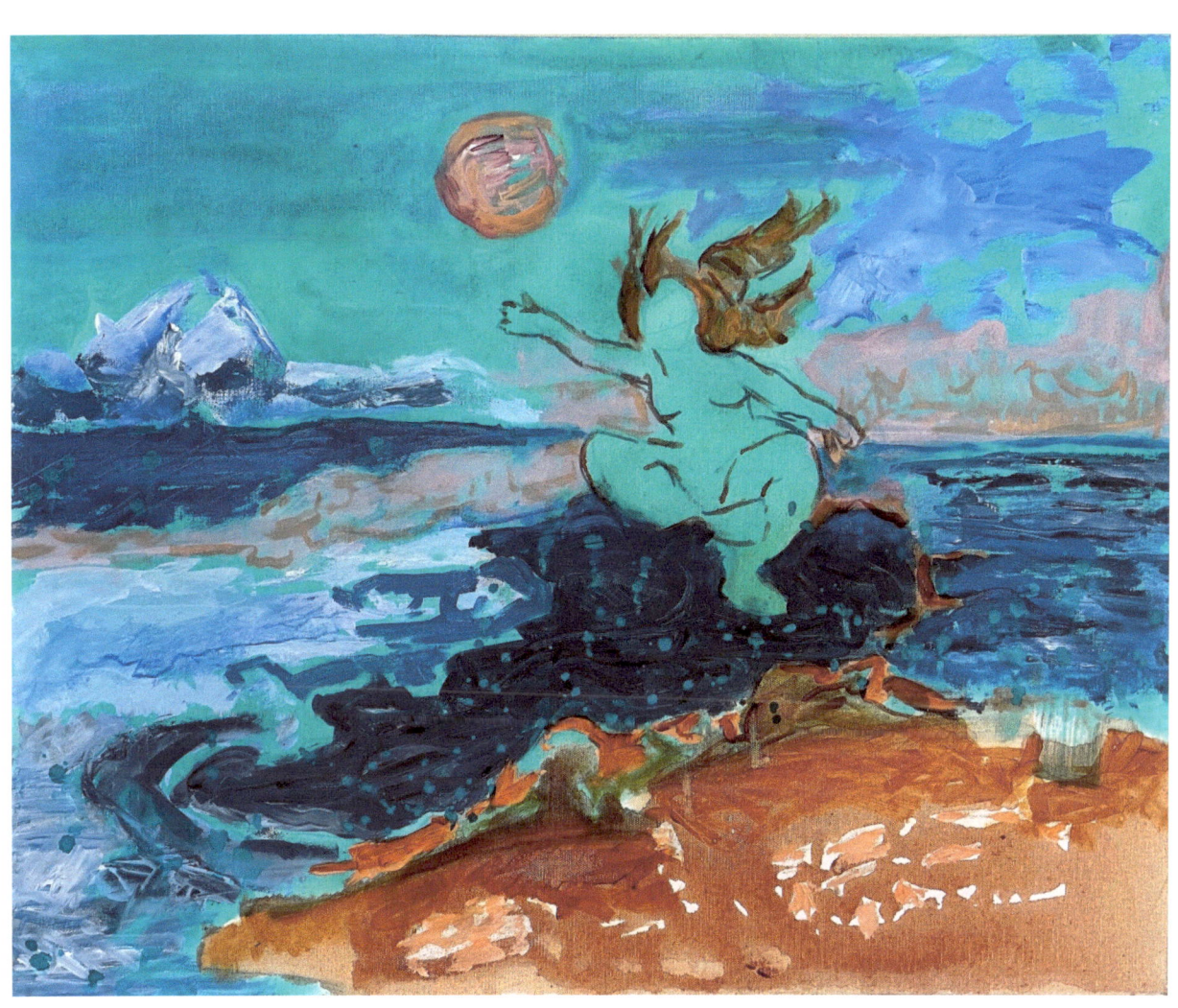

"Creative Spirit"

Strength, Wisdom, and Nature.
Yearning for an unedited life.
Yet persona and shadow are still masked.
A window: escape, clarity.
A dog: growing more confident, more present.

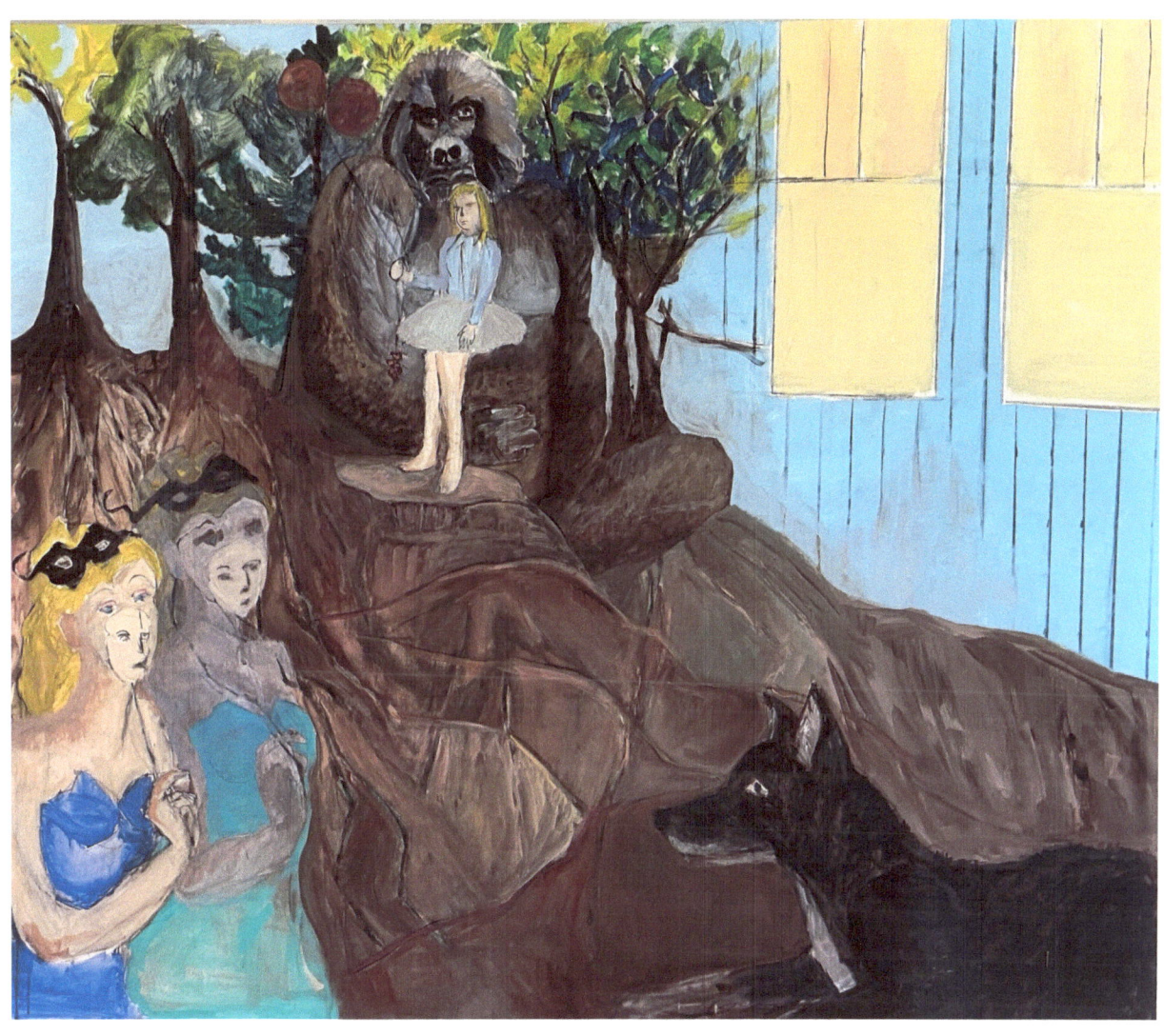

"Gorilla Spirit Reigns"

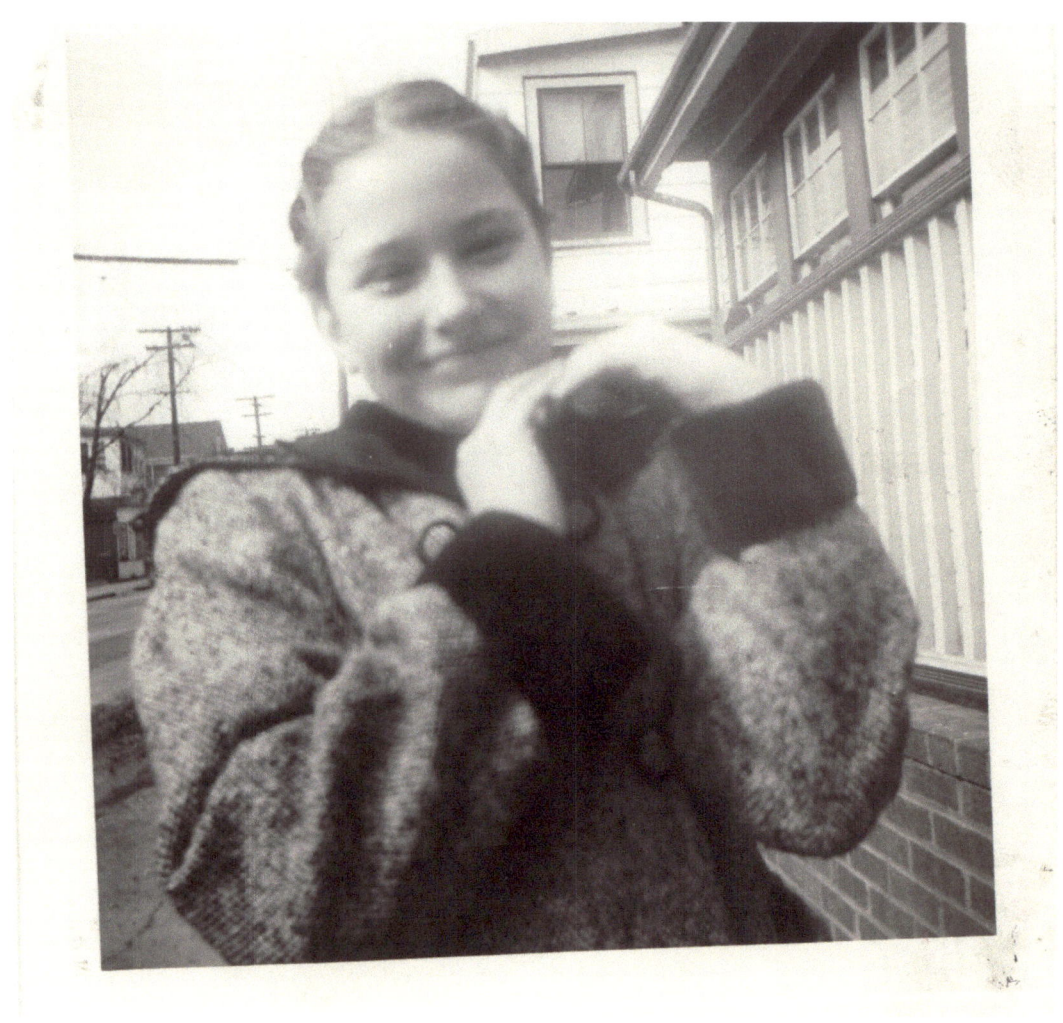

Intergenerational Communication

Feral. Free roaming.
I was finally finding the right pack to run with.
And hearing my grandfather Bill's and Grandma Rose's
healing messages.

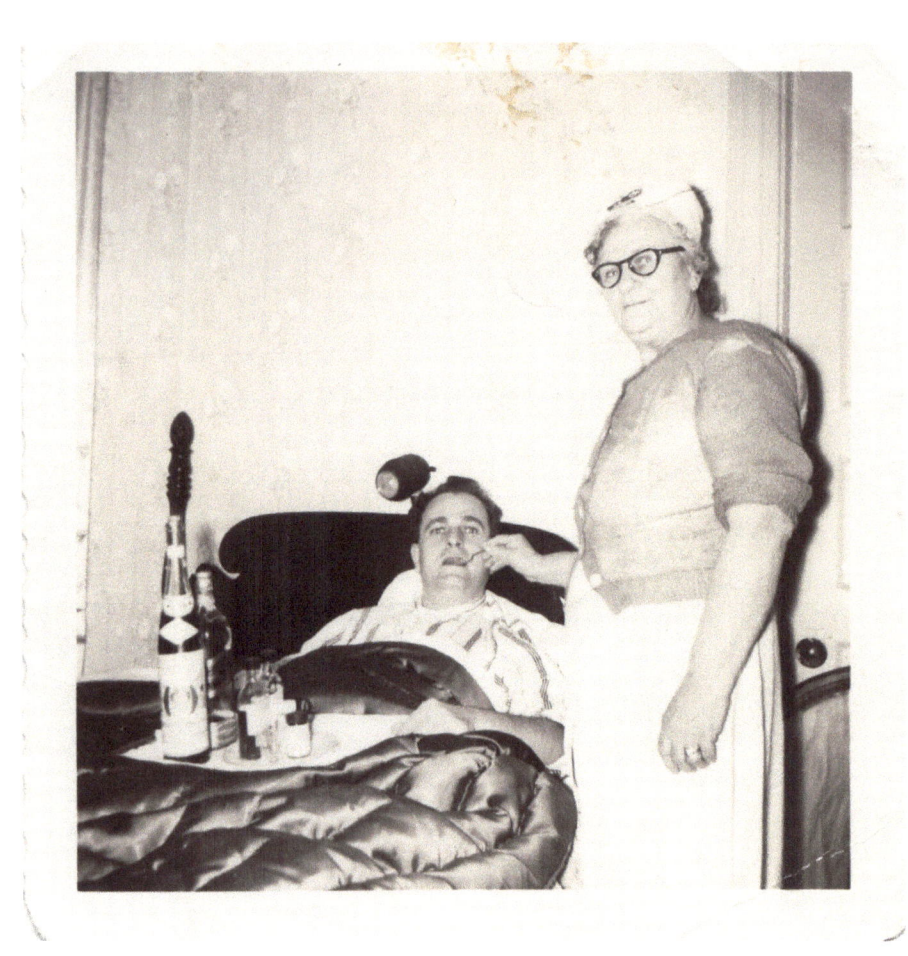

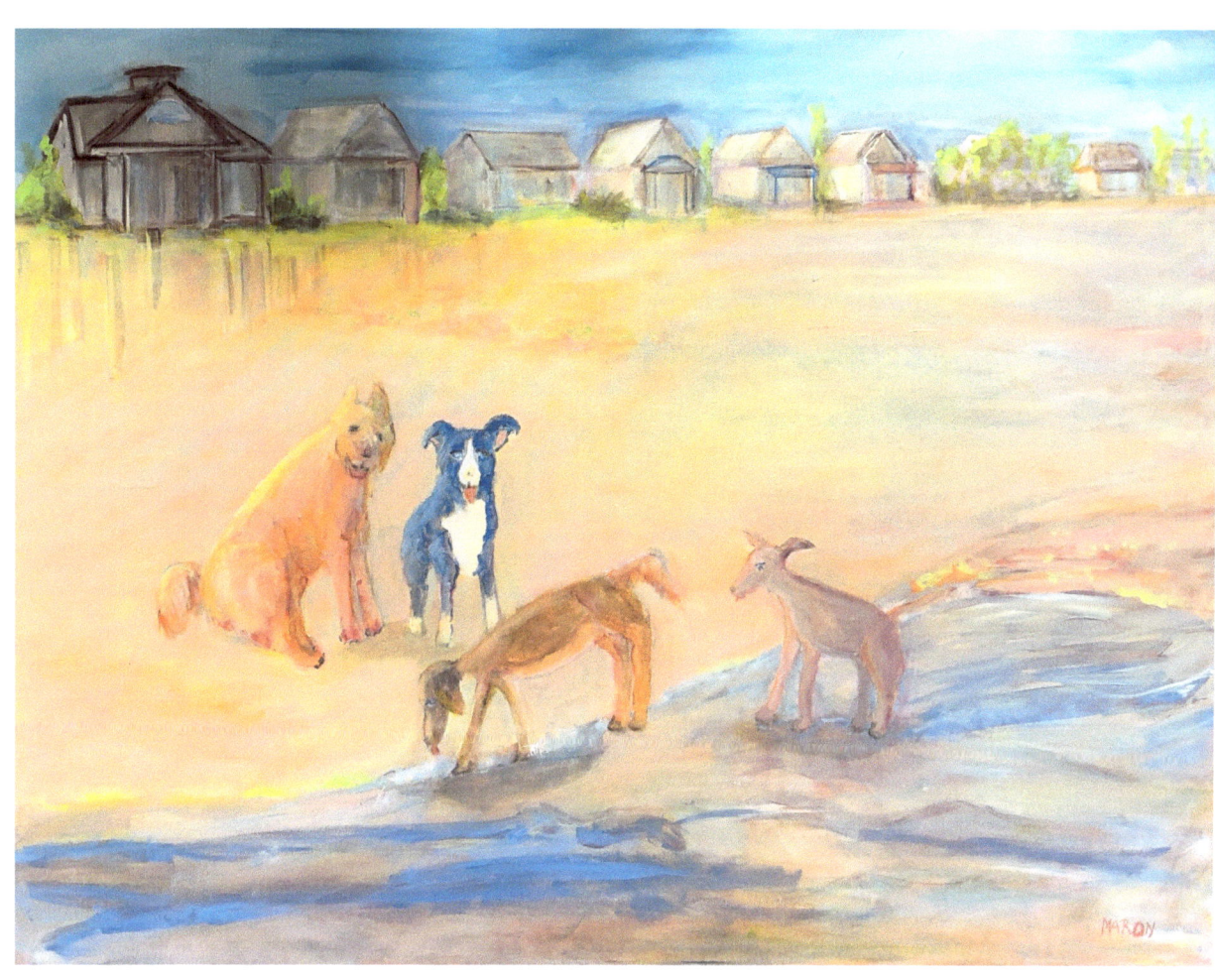

"Running Free"

Late Stone Age stele are found throughout Europe.
Lifesize, male and female.
Do they speak the same language?
Communiques passed along miles and miles
from generation to generation.
Some wisdom. Some crap. Some fears.
Hunter-gatherer cell phones.

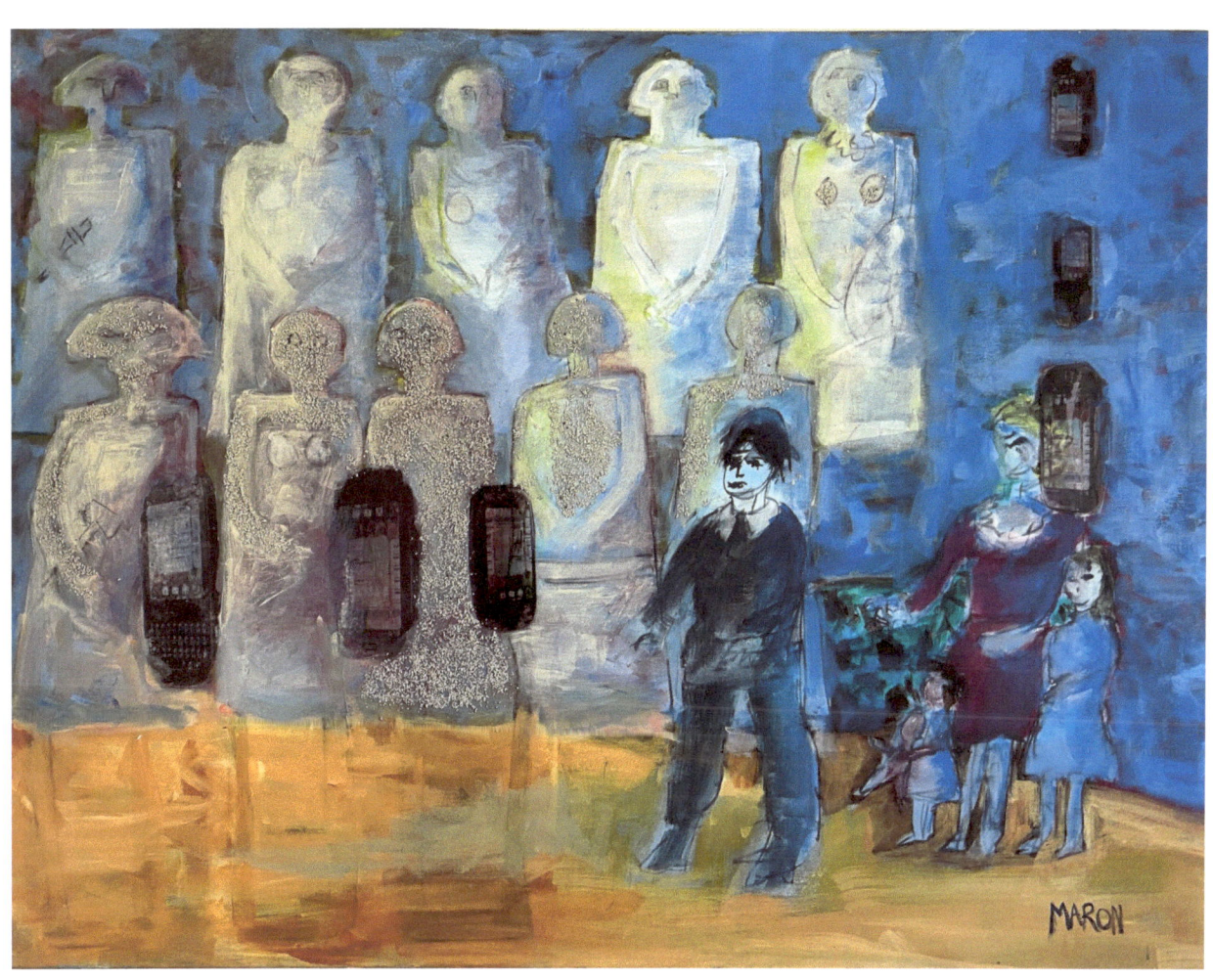

"Mapping Messages (from the Neolithic to the Digital Age)"

Larry

Larry Soll was a microbiologist at Harvard Medical School. We have now been married for forty-seven years and have eight grandchildren.

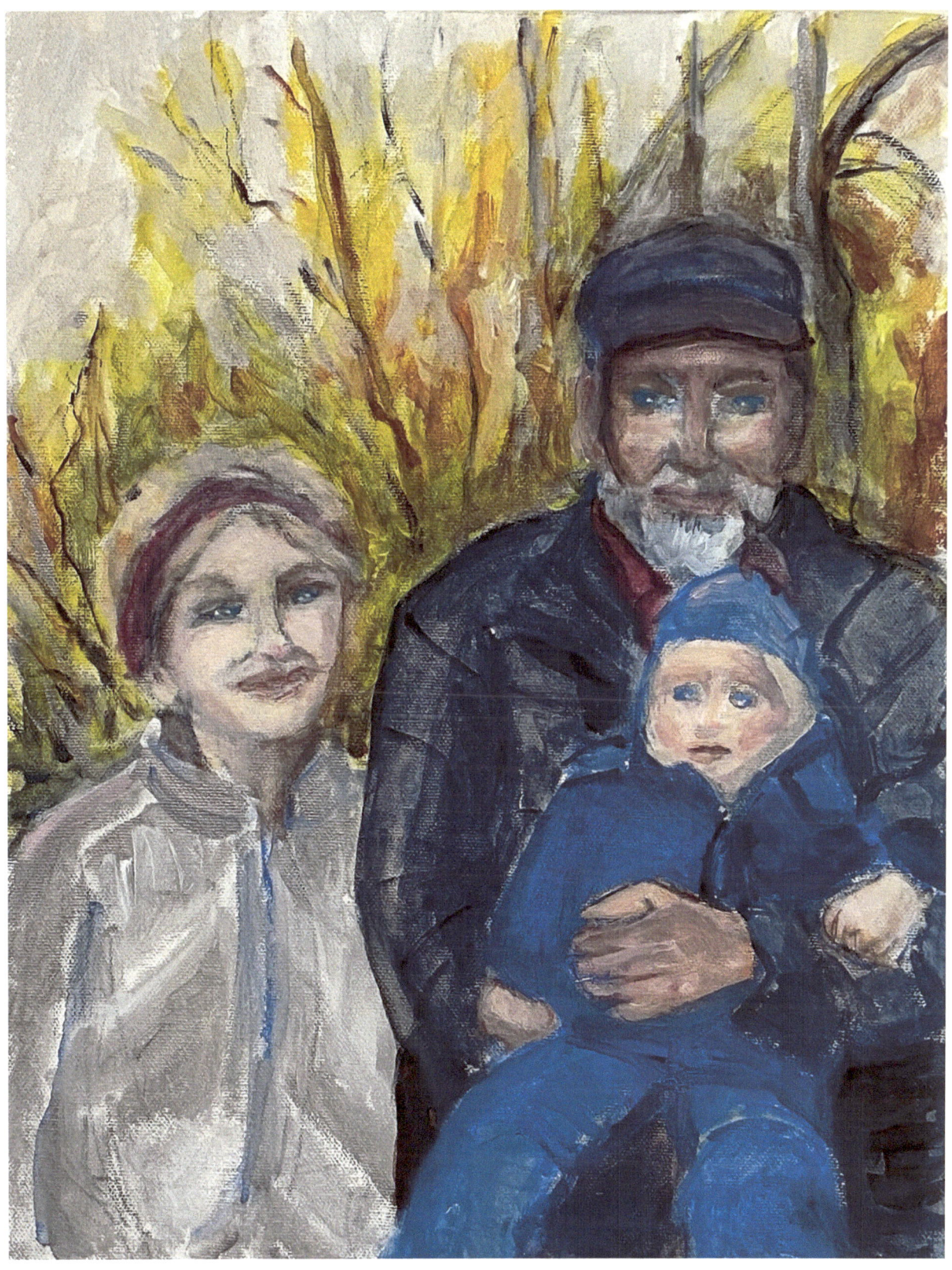

"Beckett's First Trip to the Zoo"

Contentment.
No longer fractured.
Out of the shadows.
Removing the mask.

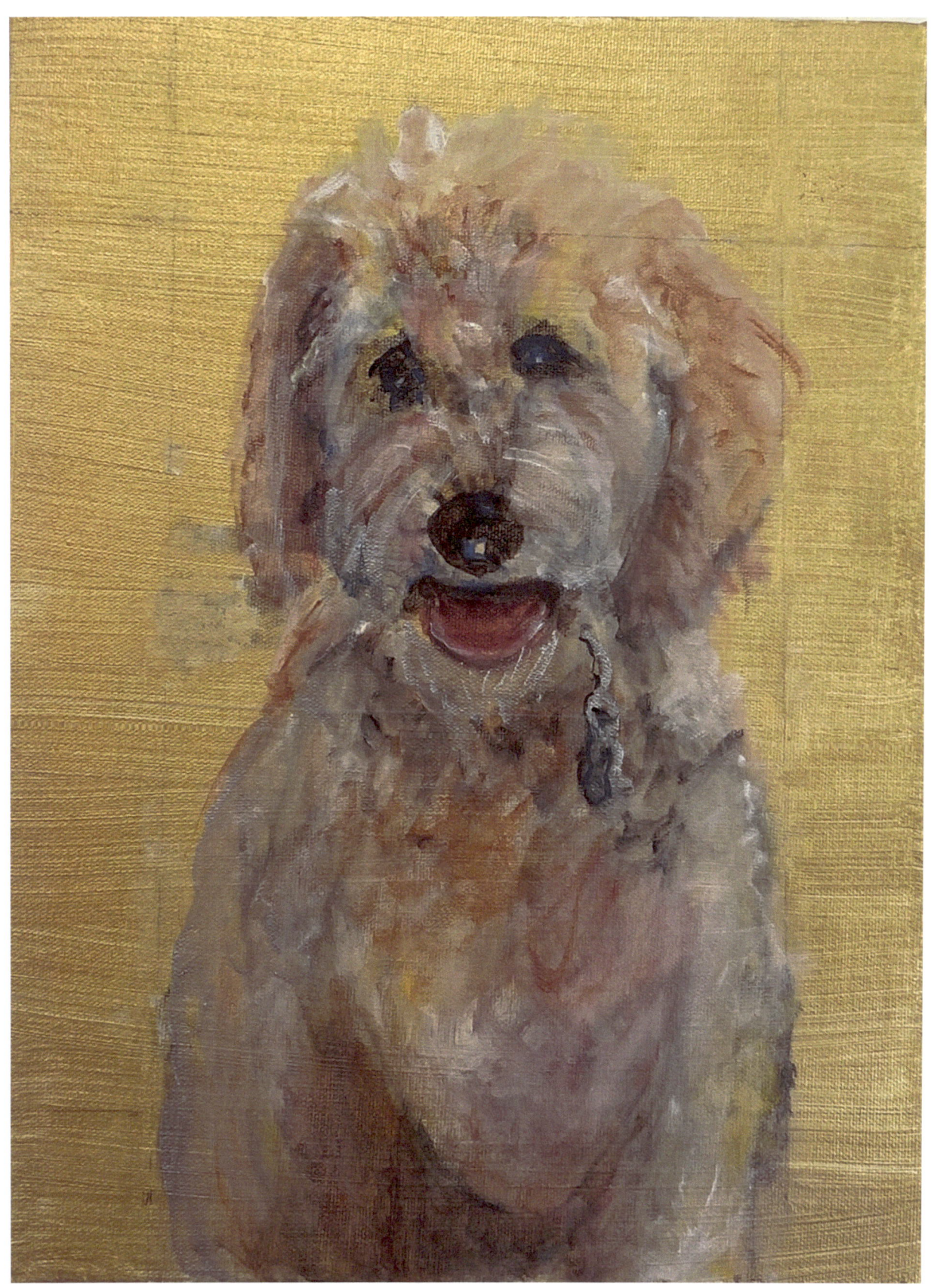

"Bela"

Life's geometry.
The seasons come and go.

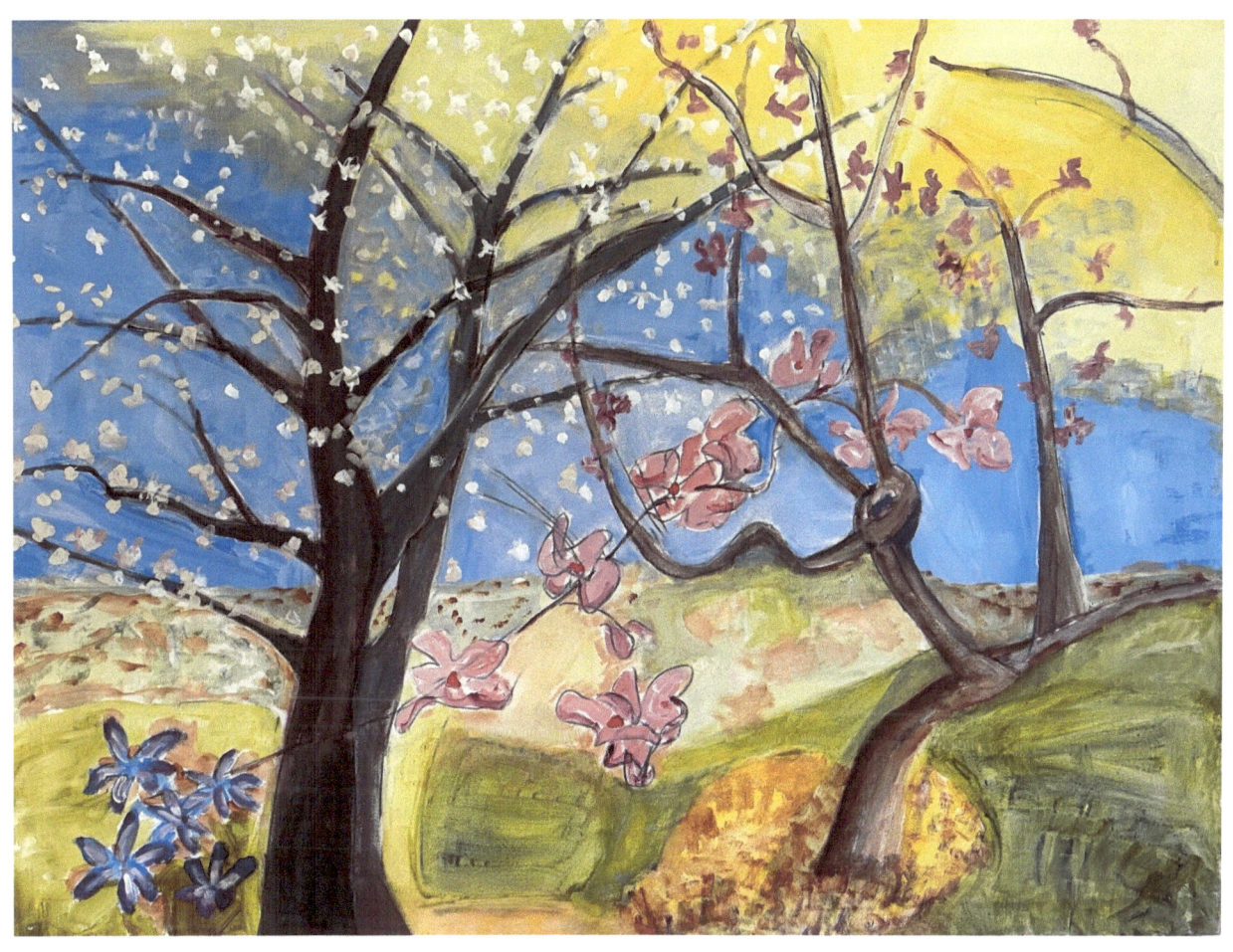

"Spring"

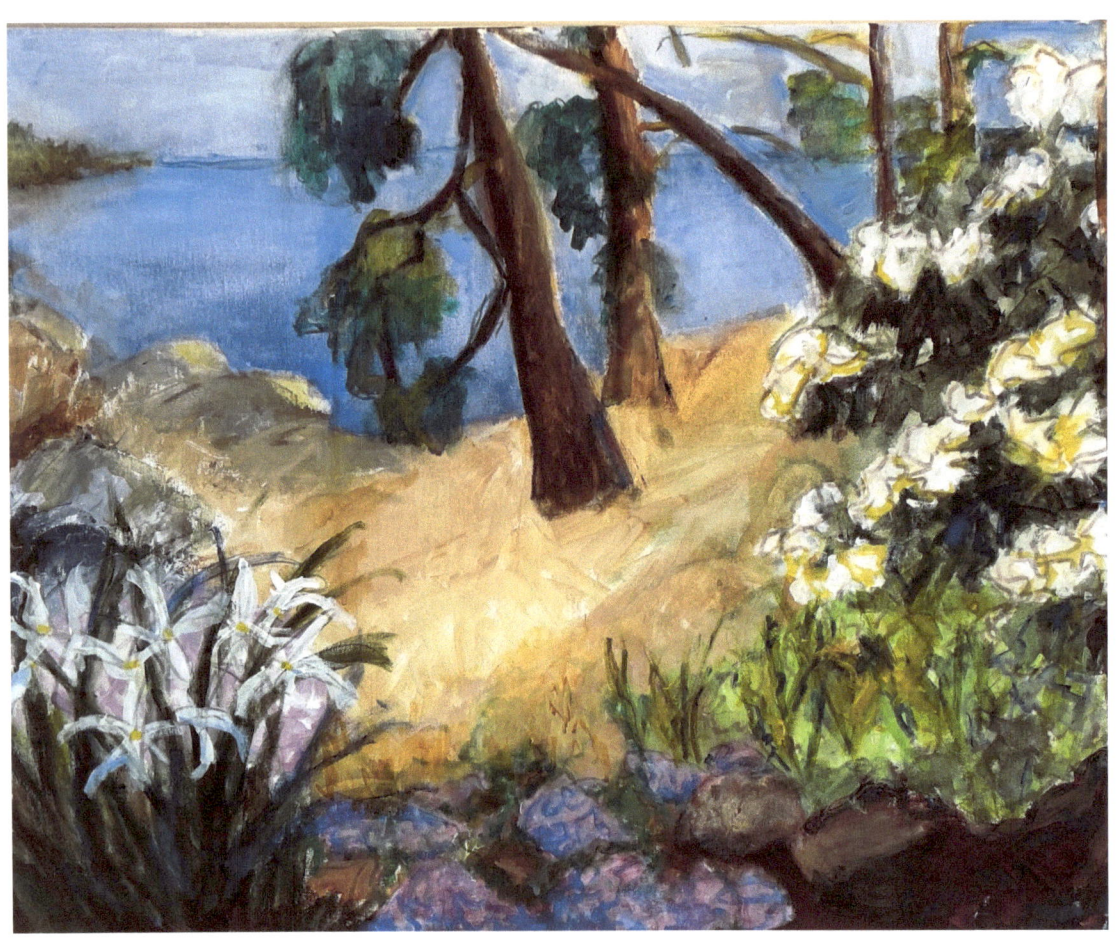

"Summer"

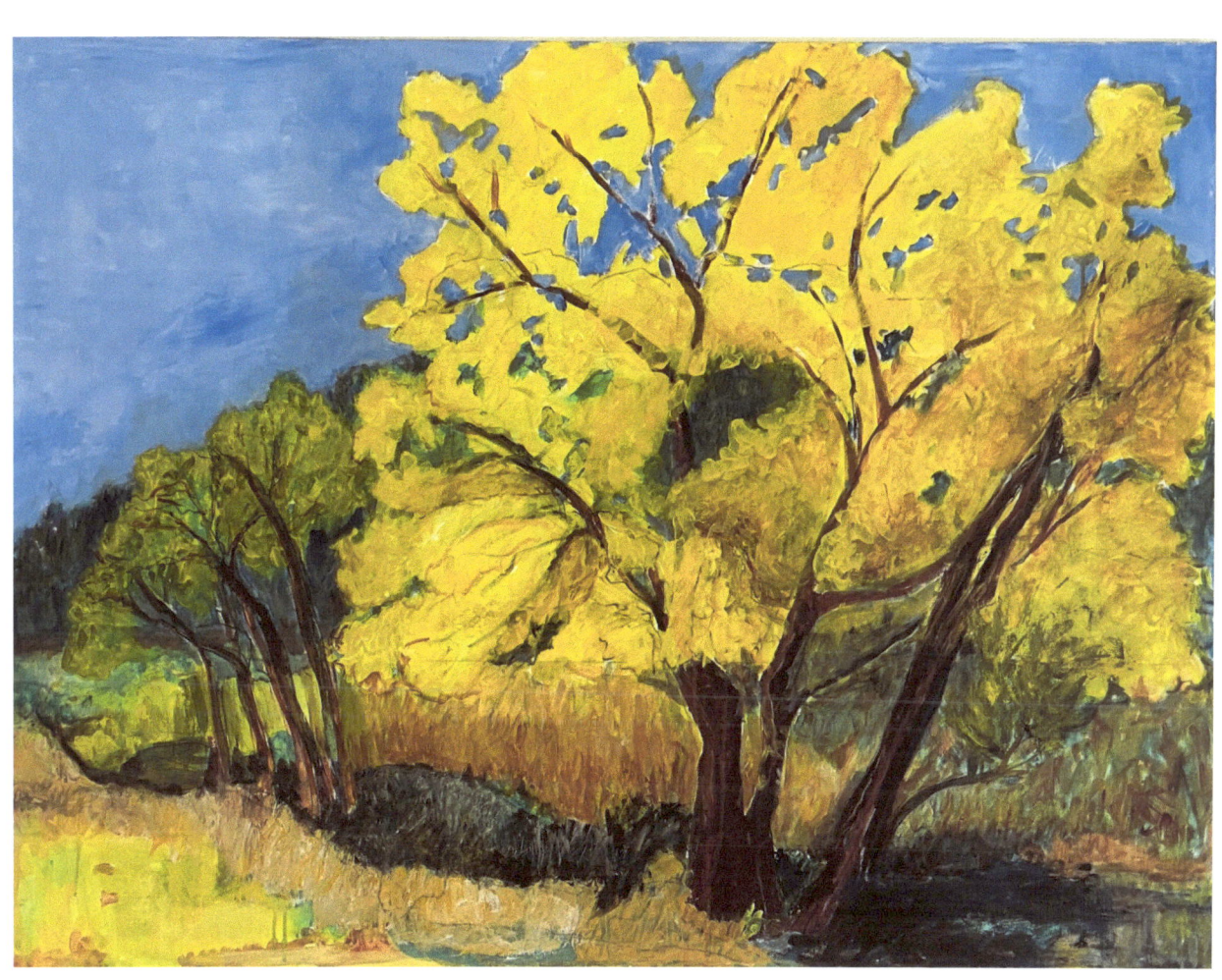

"Autumn"

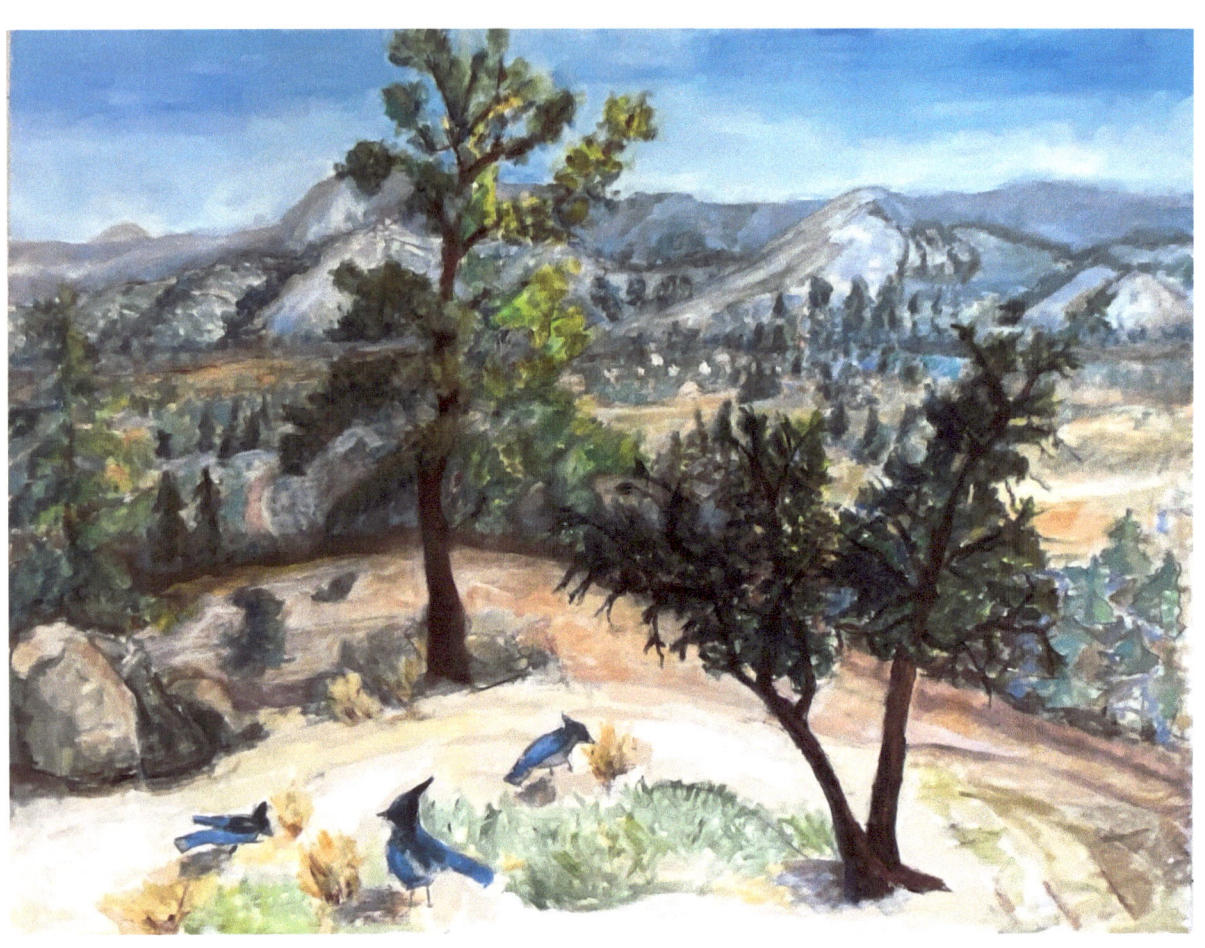

"Winter"

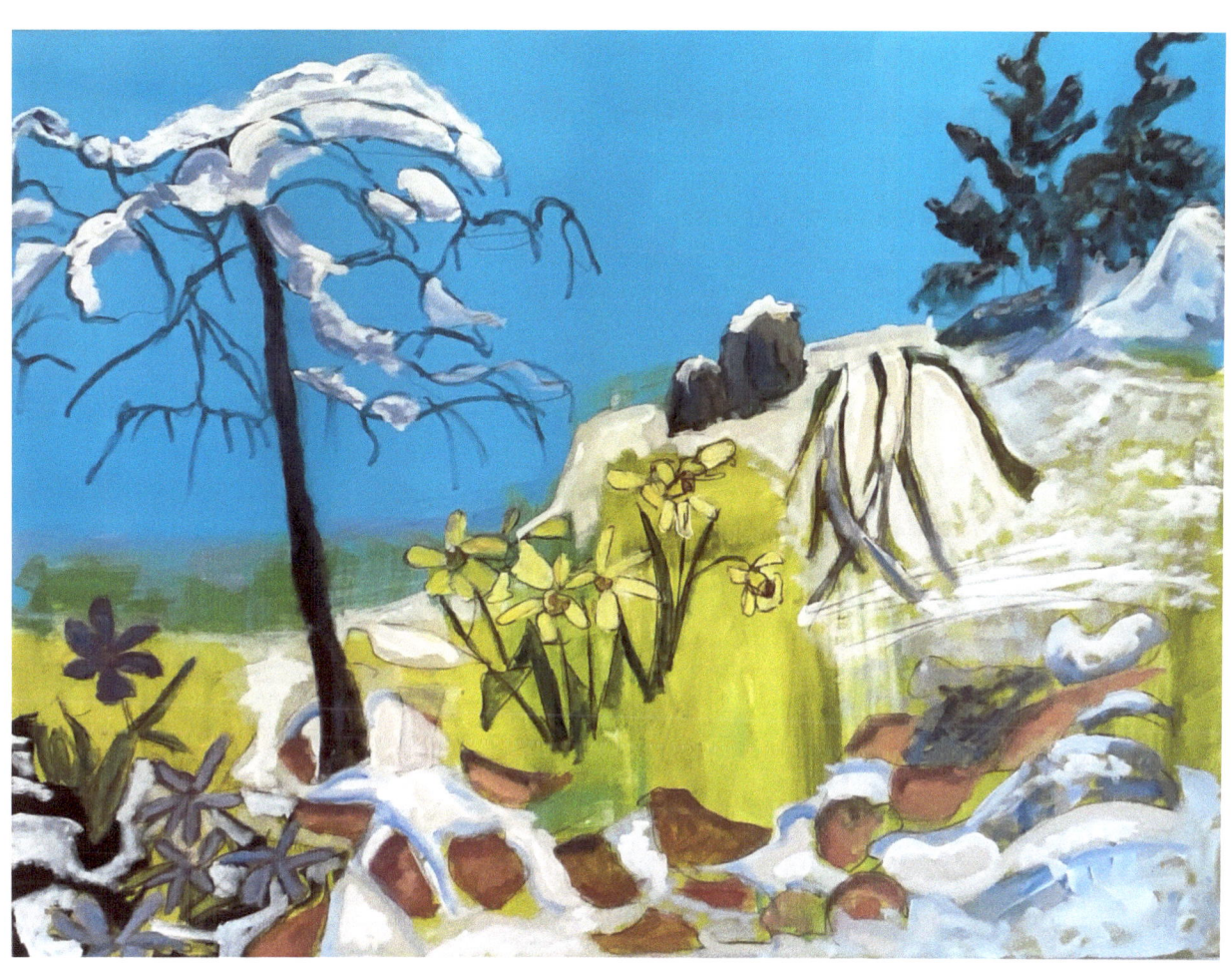

"Winter into Spring"

Photographs

PAGE 2
    Nancy, 10. The Ansco camera was a Christmas gift from her father.

PAGE 8
    Grandmother Rose at age 16, with her first-born son, Nancy's uncle, ca. 1912.

PAGE 10
    Nancy's father with her sister Lana and her doll, her constant companion.

PAGE 26
    Mother posing as a ballerina.

PAGE 28
    Nancy, 10.

PAGE 32
    Family vacation. Left to right: Mother, Nancy, Father. Sister Lana standing with her hand on the buffalo.

PAGE 34
    Double exposure. Lana running through the photo setup.

PAGE 36
    High-school graduation. Nancy on the far left.

PAGE 44
    Nancy and her three sons. Bill, 4, Jon and Joel, 8 months.

PAGE 46
    High-school musical, *A Funny Thing Happened on the Way to the Forum*. Nancy, left, with her best friend.

PAGE 50
    Nancy on the street in front of her house. Grandmother's house is in the background.

PAGE 52
    Mother Rose pretending to be a nurse feeding medicine to Nancy's uncle. She placed a tray on the bed with a liquor bottle as medicine.

Checklist

"Lupine and Madrona Tree
 on San Juan Island"
2015
Acrylic on Canvas
24"x20"
[FRONTISPIECE]

"Emergence"
1995
Raspberry Alabaster
16"x13"x10"
[DEDICATION PAGE]

"Though the Window"
2003
Oil on Canvas
30"x24"
[P. 3]

"Grandmother's Parlor"
2002
Oil on Canvas
24"x30"
[P. 5]

"Fairy Godmother Bowl"
2004
Painted Ceramic Bowl
Dimensions variable
[P. 7]

"Sunroom- My House"
2002
Oil on Canvas
24"x30"
[P. 11]

"My Father's Chair"
2002
Oil on Canvas
24"x30"
[P. 13]

"The Father I Wish I Had"
n.d.
Ballpoint Pen
11"x14"
[P. 15]

"Mother #1"
2003
Oil on Canvas
14"x11"
[P. 17]

"Mother #2"
2003
Oil on Canvas
14"x11"
[P. 19]

"Clash / Crash"
2012
Acrylic on Canvas
24"x30"
[P. 21]

"Mother #3"
2003
Oil on Canvas
14"x11"
[P. 23]

"Mother #4"
2003
Oil on Canvas
14"x11"
[P. 25]

"Try and Make me"
2019
Acrylic on Canvas
14"x11"
[P. 29]

"Family Circus"
2010
Acrylic on Canvas
30"x40"
[P. 31]

"Self Portrait"
2008
Oil On Canvas
14"x11"
[P. 35]

"Big Alone #1"
2012
Acrylic on Canvas
24"x20"
[P. 37]

"Big Alone #2"
2008
Acrylic on Canvas
14"x11"
[P. 39]

"Sunday Afternoon"
2007
Oil on Canvas
16"x 20"
[P. 41]

"Mother and Child"
n.d.
Graphite on Paper
11"x11½"
[P. 43]

"Creative Spirit"
2016
Acrylic on Canvas
24"x 30"
[P. 47]

"Gorilla Spirit Reigns"
2008
Oil on Canvas
60"x72"
[P. 49]

"Running Free"
2015
Acrylic on Canvas
24"x30"
[P. 53]

"Mapping Messages
　　　(from the Neolithic to the Digital Age)"
2010
Acrylic on Canvas
24"x30"
[P. 55]

"Beckett's First Trip to the Zoo"
2020
Acrylic on Canvas
14"x11"
[P. 57]

"Bela"
2020
Acrylic on Canvas
16"x12"
[P. 59]

from *The Seasons*
"Spring"
"Summer"
"Autumn"
"Winter"
"Winter into Spring"
All: 2016
All: Acrylic on Canvas
All: 36"x48"
[PP. 61 - 65]

"Lupine and Manzanita on San Juan Island"
2006
Acrylic on Canvas
24"x20"
Collection of David Casper
[ENDPIECE]

Gratitude

My thanks first and foremost go to my sons, my late sister, Lana – who've loved my art and have hung all kinds of strange or wonderful paintings on their walls – and Larry Soll, my partner in life, love, and real estate for forty-seven years. He is my font of knowledge and all good things, as well as the principal photographer for this book. John Lueder and David Casper also contributed photos: thank you!

I am profoundly grateful for my friendship with the late Margaretta Gilboy, a major, nationally recognized artist and good friend who gave me support and encouragement, and who passed away in 2017, leaving those who loved her bereft of her presence, but not of her spirit.

And I thank my extraordinary art teachers, Joe Miller in Friday Harbor, Madeleine Weiner, who taught me stone sculpture at Denver's Art Students League Marble / Marble Symposium, and Sally Elliott, who taught painting at the University of Colorado-Boulder. My art buddies in Colorado and Taos, Susan Behrendt and Lynn Myers, and on San Juan Island, Beth Hetrick, Becky Kilpatrick and Lisa Nash Lawrence.

Geometry of Life: A Memoir in Painting would not exist without Jennifer Heath. One day, in September 2019, Jennifer was visiting my studio to catch up on art and social matters, big and small. I showed her a new painting of a little girl who reminded me of myself as a kid. Jennifer mused that perhaps many of my paintings were autobiographical and, with that in mind, we reviewed my Magnum Opus. She was right! The paintings are about my life. "We should write a book," she said. And so we did. Jennifer curated the paintings and photographs, conceptualized the flow of the "story," and helped shape the narrative. I am honored to have her as a mentor, co-producer, and friend.

Finally, gratitude to my parents to whom I owe the lessons of grace and liberation in adversity.

–Nancy Maron
Boulder, Colorado
2020

Art Certificate

This certifies that

Nancy Canavan

has been awarded *First Prize* at the

Annual Revere School Art Exhibition

Grade *IV* School *Paul Revere*

Given at Revere Public Schools

Revere, Massachusetts this *15th* day of *May* 19*48*

Arthur H. Gavin — Arthur H. Gavin
Art Director of the Revere Public Schools

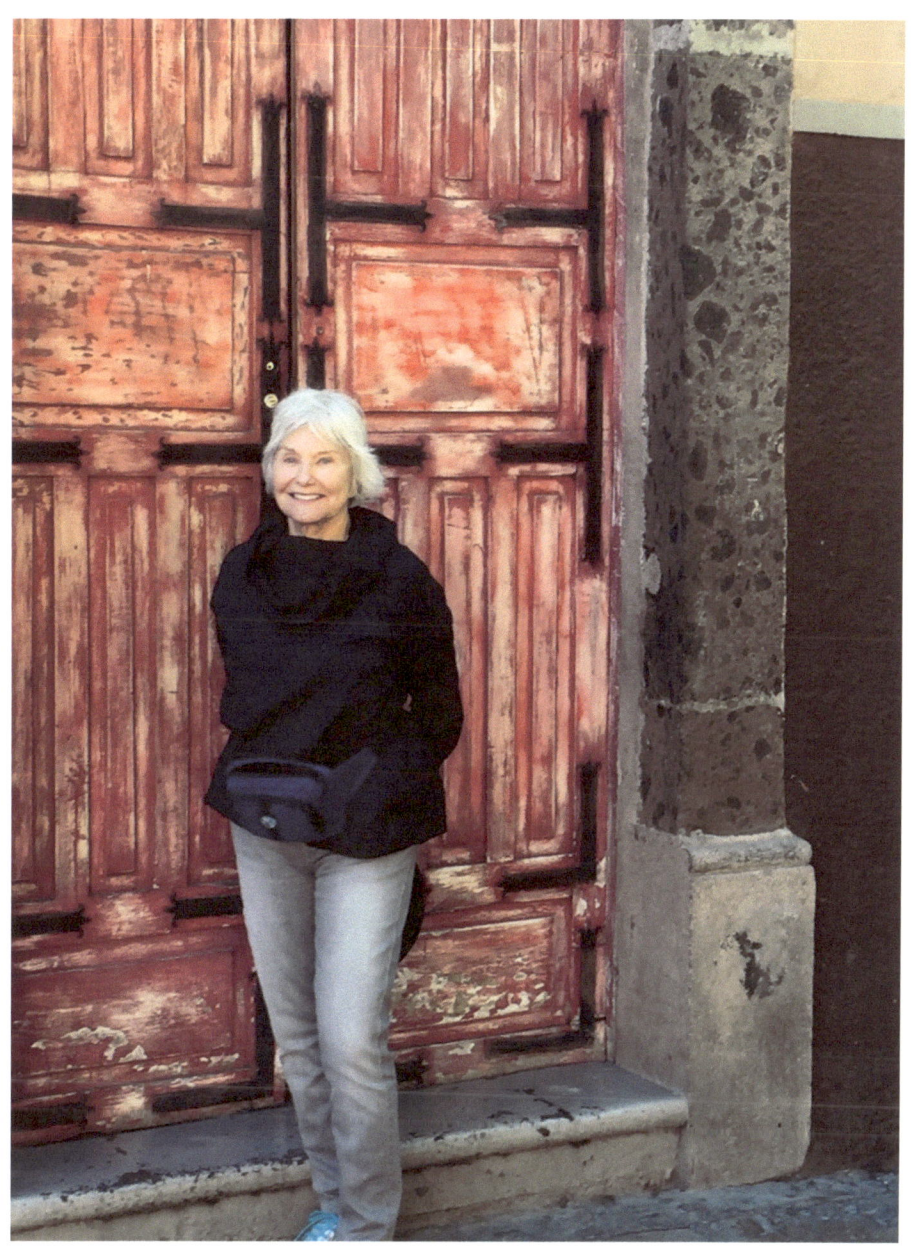

Nancy Maron is originally from Boston and moved to Boulder in the 1970s to begin a career working with the court systems nationally and with state government, eventually running the Colorado Job Training program. During that time, she enrolled at the University of Denver, receiving a doctorate in Sociology in 1990. A few years later – with her three sons grown – painting and sculpture became her primary focuses. She studied at Denver's Art Students League, the Loveland Academy of Art, and the University of Colorado, among others. Today, she splits the year between Boulder and San Juan Island, Washington, and tries to capture the landscapes in oil and acrylics. Her studios in Boulder and San Juan Island are open by appointment.

nancymaronart.com

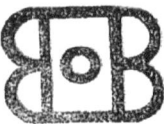

About Baksun Books & Arts

The mission of Baksun Books & Arts (fiscally sponsored by the Boulder County Arts Alliance) is to produce imaginative projects, publish books of poetry and prose, and curate art exhibitions (frequently on behalf of social and environmental justice), accompanied by comprehensive exhibition catalogues. Baksun attempts to approach and examine issues from as many creative and interactive angles as possible in the firm belief that the arts can influence lasting change.

Baksun was founded by Jennifer Heath in 1992 as a small press dedicated to de-commodifying the word and, in 1994, began creating educational and topical art exhibitions as well. It has reached thousands of all ages through diverse activities in museums, galleries, grassroots organizations, neighborhoods, schools, children's groups, libraries, and the Internet. Baksun brings together strategies for confronting today's issues, illustrating and contextualizing them to highlight the beauty of our natural and cultural gifts and resources, and to heal. The arts not only "speak truth to power," but uphold that truth and carry it forward.

Selected Recent Baksun Publications

Where a Piece of Me is Torn Away, poems by Juliet Carpenter, 2020

The Last Tourist in Bali, stories by Tree Bernstein, 2020

Murmurations: Wingèd Beings Sacred and Profane, exhibition catalogue, 2019

Imaginary Maps: Expeditions to Uncover Apocryphal, Unsubstantiated, and Forbidden Places, exhibition catalogue, 2018

How I Learned to Cook: An Artist's Life, by Barbara Shark, 2018

Addled Smoke Material: Collaborative Poems 1972-2017, by Jack Collom and Reed Bye, 2017

Celebration! A History of the Visual Arts in Boulder, exhibition catalogue, 2016

"The Map Is not the Territory": Parallel Paths – Palestinians, Native Americans, Irish, exhibition catalogue, 2015

Water, Water Everywhere: Paeon to a Vanishing Resource, exhibition catalogue, 2014

Forthcoming: *OnWORDS! Boulder's Book Arts Legacy*, exhibition catalogue, 2020

BAKSUN BOOKS & ARTS
1838 PINE STREET
BOULDER, CO. 80302 USA

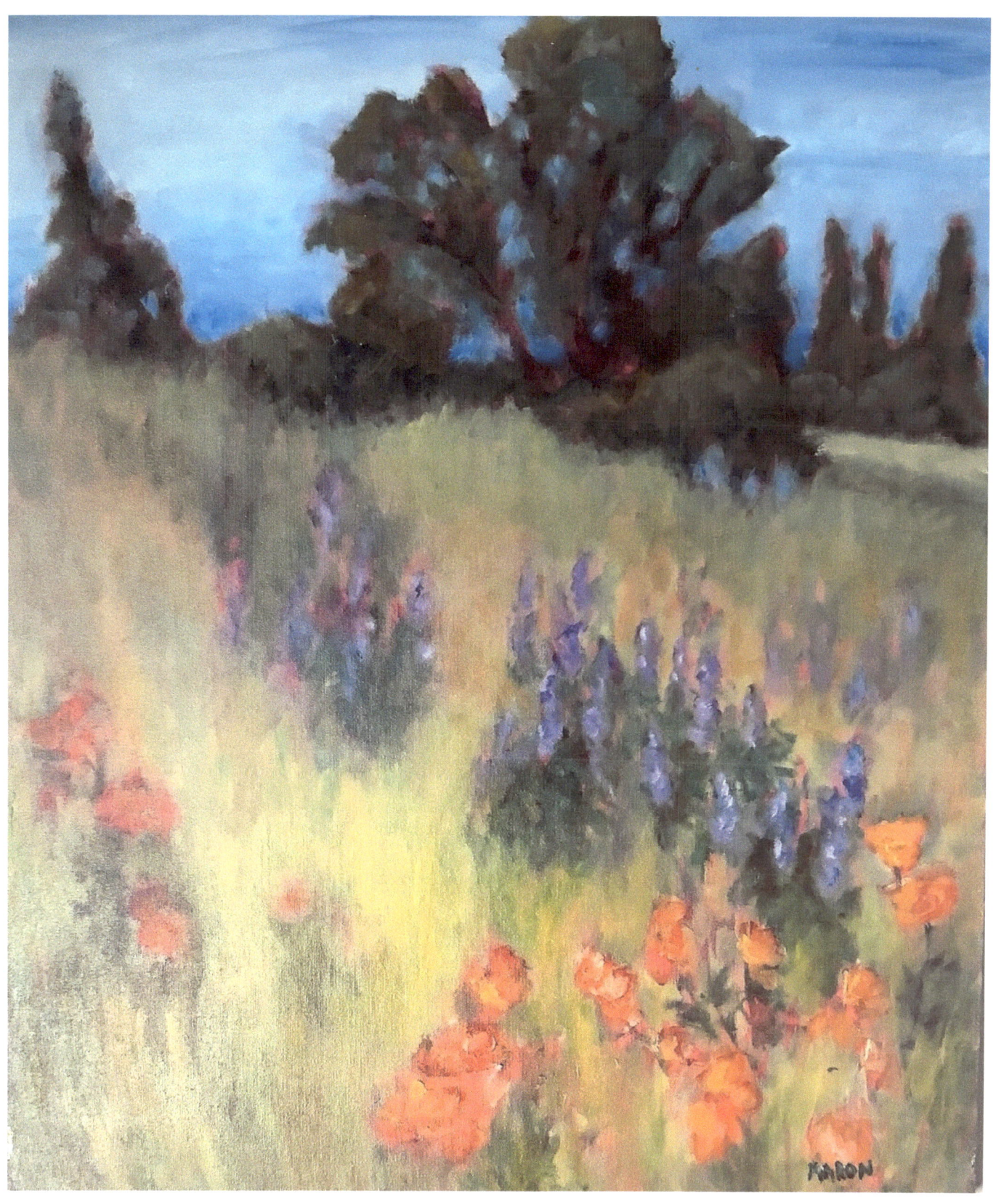

"Lupine and Manzanita Tree on San Juan Island"

www.ingramcontent.com/pod-product-compliance
Lightning Source LLC
Chambersburg PA
CBHW051159220526
45473CB00003B/828